Dead Jokes

Getting the Lapsed Laugh

Kevin Frushour

This is a work of non-fiction. Some names, characters, events, and places are real. Any resemblance to actual persons or events shouldn't be much of a surprise.

Published by Hartwix Press

Cover artwork by Amy Frushour Kelly

ISBN: 979-8-9949165-0-6 (eBook)
ISBN: 979-8-9949165-1-3 (softcover)
ISBN: 979-8-9949165-2-0 (hardcover)

Author's Note

Generally people don't put in a content warning for a book of jokes. They just mention on the cover that it is either "clean" or "dirty". However… this is a historical work just as much as it is a joke book, and I want to make sure all readers are forewarned:

These are jokes from history, and some of the topics aren't pleasant. This book uses some sensitive language for the purposes of clarity. The topics ahead can involve references to slurs, stereotypes, death, abuse, suicide, questionable consent and sexual assault.

Not *every* joke here is like that, but some absolutely are. Humor can be – if you'll pardon the expression – funny like that.

Contents

Preface 7

What is a Joke?.. 15

How the Jokes Were Chosen 19

Changes to the Jokes.. 29

Categories 39

Technology: Communication 41

Technology: Appliances and Devices...................... 109

Technology: Traveling.. 147

Events: 1850-1900 207

Events: 1900-1925 215

Events: 1925-1950 229

Events: 1950-1975 251

Events: 1975-2000 267

Culture..285

Afterword 337

Acknowledgements..338

Thanks 341

Bibliography 343

Index 347

Preface

When humor becomes outdated, it dies a quiet death.

Comedians want their audience to laugh, not scratch their heads. They see an old joke in a book and either they don't get it, or they do get it but don't want to go through the trouble of setting up a lot of background for a single laugh. When publishers go through old joke books to compile updated books, they see the old humor, realize that no one will get it now, and the gag is quickly excluded and forgotten.

Goodbye, joke. We hardly knew ye.

I love humor, especially short jokes. My grandparents loved them, and my parents loved them. I can't recall exactly when I personally started loving them the way I do, but there was lots of fun along the way.

One memory I have as a child is of my father telling this one to my mother:

> *Three Mexican brothers living in America decided to make a good old-fashioned Mexican dinner like their mother used to make. Pablo was asked to get the nacho cheese, but he found there was no cheese to be had in stores— there was a national cheese shortage! As Pablo was walking home empty-handed, he saw a big government truck handing out blocks of cheese, but it ran out while he was waiting in line to get some.*

Not wanting to disappoint his brothers, he grabbed a block of cheese from a man and ran. The man gave chase for a few blocks, yelling, but finally gave up. When Pablo got home, exhausted, his brothers opened the box and said it wasn't nacho cheese. Pablo replied "It is! The big guy I stole it from chased me down the street yelling 'Dat's nacho cheese!'"

I remember sitting there, absorbing the punchline. "Nacho" sounds like "not your"— I'd never thought about it before. I continued to think about it for a few days. Do cheese shortages really happen like that?[1] Why didn't Pablo's brothers already know about the cheese shortage? Exactly what kind of cheese did Pablo bring home anyway? Why would he think the man chasing him down the street would be yelling the specific type of cheese that had been stolen?

These were all signs of a developing humorist, picking a funny story apart and trying to understand every aspect.

I grew up in a progressive home and my sister and I were allowed to ask about anything we were curious about. We were allowed to swear (so long as we knew it was only at home) and hear dirty jokes. We knew where babies came from at an early age, so the idea of sex in jokes wasn't a shock to us as it was in other families. One time when I was

---

[1] No, but in the 1980's an excess of milk in the United States lead to converting much of that surplus into "government cheese", then distributing it to food banks and charities. The saying "getting government cheese" has become a term for being on public assistance since.

10, my friends and I were looking at a copy of the men's magazine *Playboy* one of us had found. I liked the pictures, absolutely— but the joke page! The cartoons! Wow!

I learned the hard way that not everyone enjoys a dirty joke, let alone one told by a child, and that some of those jokes which seemed innocent to me were actually inappropriate or outright racist. I had always assumed the people living around me were "normal people" and appreciated the humor —just like my parents. My family had brought me up to accept everyone but, being a child, I incorrectly assumed that the stereotypical characters in the jokes must not really exist, or they lived in some far away land or time.

Needless to say… they didn't. The Jewish folks, black folks, and Polish folks were all right there in my childhood hometown of 1980s Toledo, Ohio. I told a few jokes to the wrong adults, at the wrong time. I didn't get punished, but I remember the distinct change in the manner of the adult afterwards and sometimes they'd even have a word with my parents. While I was young and naive, it was a lesson to me of how humor can hurt just as well as make people laugh.

I grew up, and I learned to be more careful. Consider your audience, pick a matching joke. If you aren't sure if the group can handle a certain joke, either don't tell it or ask first— even when asking might take a little of the "zing" out of a punchline.

When Jokes Die

The most popular, timeless humor and comedy routines are slice-of-life quips about dating, courtship, marriage, sex, and raising children. The ones referring to occupations, such as teachers, farmers, lawyers, and politicians are all understood by everyone, and easily updated to today. Those topics haven't changed and the humor hasn't changed.

What intrigued me, over my years of loving humor, was that some jokes expire.

I was with my family, in the car with my grandmother. We were going to dinner somewhere, and I was probably about 7 or 8 years old, early 1980s. I asked if she could tell me a joke, and she said she had one, but I probably wouldn't get it. I asked for it anyway, and she told me a version of this:

> *A man and his wife were on an ocean voyage when the wife unexpectedly passed away. They held a burial at sea.*
>
> *The next night the husband kept hearing a ghostly voice whispering "It floats... it floats..." and the man just froze in bed, listening in fear.*
>
> *The next night, the same. "It floats... it floats..."*
>
> *On the third night again came the voice, "It floats... it floats..." and he whispered in terror "...What floats?"*
>
> *The voice said, "Ivory, the soap that floats!"*

Looking at my confused expression, my grandmother explained that Ivory brand bar soap floated in the bathtub instead of sinking, and the old slogan for it was "Ivory, the soap that floats." I had indeed not known that but was also even more confused because as a child in the 1980s I was more familiar with Ivory as a brand of dishwashing liquid than as a brand of bar soap.

I got older, and my own library of jokes increased. With that, I told some that I myself had to explain to people. For example, the Yugo was a car heavily marketed in the United States in the 1980s as an inexpensive, everyman's car.

I really liked this next joke which I first heard in high school in the early 1990s:

Q: How do you double the value of a Yugo?
A: Fill the gas tank.

After a few years I would start to tell this joke and before I could even begin the punchline, people were interrupting me asking "What's a Yugo?", breaking up the joke's flow. I had to update the joke with more modern cheap car names but this got hard to keep up with so I dropped the joke eventually.

This idea of jokes fading into obscurity kept tugging at my brain. I was certain someone else must have covered this before! Unfortunately the internet, which I could usually coax into taking me straight to where I wanted it to go, began to fail me.

I searched for "old jokes" and only found humor about getting old.

I searched for "dead jokes" and only found humor about death.

I searched for "history jokes" and I found humor about history… but not humor no one would get.

I searched for "humor of yesteryear" and got things like "Ten jokes from 1910 still as funny today!" … but I didn't want the ones that were still as funny today; I wanted the ones that were only funny in 1910!

Having come up empty online, I started to note the jokes in my repertoire that I thought younger folks wouldn't get. I combed through old books and the internet looking for quips about events, culture, and technology that were relevant in their time, but were obscure now.

I realized that I wasn't looking for specifically "old" jokes either, in the common meaning. That word can also mean stale, trite and cliché. The jokes I was looking for were so far out of the everyday public perception that they are actually new and fun, kind of like finding your grandparents old toys in the attic.

Finding them required going against the flow. As stated before, most jokes are collected for telling or publishing according to "this is funny" or "everyone will get this one." I was doing exactly the opposite of that. Giving myself a list of criteria that this humor would fall under and doing my best to stick to it.

There are two good reasons these jokes should be remembered. First, these are literally history, both in that they deal with the past, and they are "dead" jokes. They're not gone forever though. They can come back by breathing a little life into them with an explanation.

Second, some people learn best through humor. Humor can be used to add a little spice to a boring history lesson, and this book is all about tying history to humor and vice versa.

Multiple "rules of humor" were violated here. I tidied up and shortened jokes. I give a setup beforehand that sometimes spoils the punchline and then explain the punchline afterwards.

These perfectly good dead jokes deserve a little more life, and we need to make sure they stay available into the future for humorists, historians and, of course, humorous historians.

What is a Joke?

The word "joke" has a pretty lose definition: "A display of humor". For our purposes here, I'm going by what I think of as "the old-fashioned, short form, spoken word joke." It could be a very short story, a question and answer, a "knock-knock", a few sentences of observational humor, or it could be a funny poem.

A joke has two parts, which depend on each other:

> The **setup** lays down the framework for the punchline.
>
> The **punchline** which is a "twist" - an upset expectation from what was set up.

Jokes are exactly that simple. It's finding the best ones and delivering them in the right context and style to get a good response which is the hard part.

Many humor books from history are essentially collections of longer "short" stories or long-form poetry. I personally prefer rapid-fire humor books. Even though I was born long before TikToks, Reels, and the term "Too long; didn't read", I had a short attention span *before* it was cool.

A Quick History of Jokes

Jokes have existed since prehistory. Traded among people, passed along verbally. When possible, the humor would be translated and shared with other cultures. Funny stories have always been easier to translate than wordplay or puns and thus would spread more easily. Sometimes people would write the humor down and some of that written humor survived to today.

Currently, the oldest known surviving joke is Sumerian, dated 1900 BC and is, not surprisingly, a fart joke:

> *Something which has never occurred since time immemorial: a young woman did not fart in her husband's lap.*

I'm not really sure how funny that is, but there you go. I can't say I've ever experienced that myself, but it's nice to know there's something else my wife and I can try if the magic starts to fade from our relationship.

The oldest surviving proper "joke book" is in Greek, by Hierocles and Philagrius,[1] and titled *Philogelos*—"Love of Laughter." It was written somewhere around 300 AD to 700 AD. Many of the jokes in *Philogelos* are still funny, and several times I read something in it and thought "Wait— I've heard that one before! That joke is... *1,500 years old?"* Some of the humor in the book involves a Greek pun or refers to Greek culture and thus needs to be explained by scholars, but then sometimes... well, no one alive gets the joke anymore. Here's one of those jokes:

> *A scholar ordered a silversmith to prepare a lantern. When the silversmith asked how big he wanted it, he replied "Like this, for eight people!"*

---

[1] We have no idea who those authors were, or if they existed.

Is it a pun? Is it an in-joke? Was there a gesture involved, lost to time? Is it an early example of surreal humor? Sadly we don't understand it and can only guess at the meaning or give it up as unknowable.

Surviving joke books as we currently know them—long lists of short jokes—mostly date from the 1800s to the present. Many of these books were "toastmasters' books", i.e. books of anecdotes designed to give someone giving a speech some funny sayings to amuse an audience. The publicly available humor books in the first half of the century didn't get very dirty— the naughtiest you'd get is young lovers speaking of kissing while courting. Dirty jokes existed, but they were viewed as pornographic, and not something proper book sellers could publish and stock on their shelves openly.

During the 20th century, a large number of joke books were published. They were generally a cheap cash-grab: throw a bunch of jokes in a book, put in an introduction about how wonderful humor is, and publish it. It was easy money.[1] After the 1950s censorship was relaxed somewhat and books of dirty jokes could finally be published and sold in everyday bookstores.

Then the internet came along and, as all new technologies do, it both ruined everything and made it better. The old fun of "sharing the latest joke by the watercooler at work" diminished in place of email and

---

[1] It's *still* considered easy money, to the point that joke books are often listed under "oversaturated subject content" on eBook publishing sites. Anyone can cut and paste a bunch of jokes into a file and try to publish it as a joke book, selling it cheaply – it's happened so much that eBook publishers now reserve the right to reject it.

social media feeds.[1] For those of us jokesters who remember life before the internet (we're fewer every day), it felt like living through the end of an era, because now everyone we knew who liked jokes was getting the same ones from the same source, at the same time we did, before we even had the chance to share them out loud.

On the positive side it has never been easier to share humor with others— one joke can go viral on social media before everyone even sees the news story it was based on. For some people, seeing the joke/meme/whatever is what makes them look up the news story in the first place. The jokes still exist and are still being created— the method of communication has simply changed.

Throughout the history of jokes, many jokes have fallen by the wayside, forgotten – and that's our subject here. But how do we identify those jokes from all the others?

---

[1] A bit of early email history: people would format the jokes with fonts and colors to make them fun and then the emails would be forwarded so many times the jokes would become near impossible to find in the email with all the headers and footers and incompatible formatting issues.

How the Jokes Were Chosen

This is not a normal joke book which throws hundreds of jokes out at you, hoping some will stick. I had a specific goal: gathering historically outdated jokes, and for that I needed rules. I couldn't simply put in the stuff I like, or the funniest ones I read. Many great jokes ended up being excluded.

For this project I had to read thousands of jokes. This was fun at times, but also a chore because when you sit down and read book after book of short form humor you will see the same joke just worded differently over and over again - sometimes even in the same collection. I found the same issue on internet sites and humor forums.

The fact is that humans really aren't as original with jokes as they think they are. But… that just makes the original material all the more awesome. Because of this, I can guarantee that this book doesn't contain a lot of jokes you've seen a million times already in popular, mass-produced books.

Ultimately, I settled on these criteria:

- It must be about an outdated topic
- It would fall apart without an outdated topic
- It can't be recycled for a different topic
- Avoid puns unless they are very funny or apt
- Nothing after the year 1999
- No censorship

That's broadly my aim. If you find an occasional joke in here that doesn't really fall under the above categories, I claim: “artistic license,” “it’s my book,” and good old hands-over-ears “LA-LA-LA-I-CAN’T-HEAR-YOU.”

Let me explain each in more detail.

It Must Be About an Outdated Topic

What’s an outdated topic? Well… it’s a topic… and it’s… outdated.

Okay, definitions:

> **Topic:** The topic is what the joke’s punchline is about or refers to in order for the punchline to occur.

> **Outdated:** An outdated joke’s topic refers to a technology no one uses anymore, something cultural that is out-of-date, or an event far enough in the past the average listener doesn’t understand the reference.

A joke referring to an “outdated topic” often needs to be explained to the listener, much like how my grandmother had to explain the slogan for Ivory soap to me.

Quick side note here: Some of these outdated topics still exist. There are still horses used every day in some rural communities. We still fly airplanes. A product or slogan I mentioned might be reintroduced or be still around here and there. The internet is a really complex telegraph with computers on both ends. You might work in an industry or area of academia where the knowledge in this book is commonplace.

The humor that is included here is from far enough back in technology or common usage that the *average person* doesn't get it, *not that no one at all will get it anymore*. Otherwise this book would be nothing but surreal quips, like the silversmith joke from *Philogelos*.

It Would Fall Apart Without the Outdated Topic

The historical part is preferably deeply embedded in the joke, making it hard to tease out. You practically can't tell the joke without it. This helps us narrow the field down by the topic.

Let's say we were specifically looking for the topic of "blonde jokes;" a cycle of humor popular in the 1980s onwards which use the stereotypical "dumb blonde woman" as the subject. Here's one:

> *Q: How do you get a one-armed blonde out of a tree?*
> *A: Wave.*

People call this a "blonde joke" and that's fine, but we're being picky here for our purposes and this is actually a "dumb person joke" using a blonde, the punchline being that waving at whatever generic doofus/moron/ethnic stereotype/whatever would make them let go with their one hand to wave back at you, and as a result they'd fall out of the tree. The above joke has been used and reused for many years as "a one armed [dumb person]," and it's funny— but it's not specifically a blonde joke, which is what we're looking for here.

Here's an actual blonde joke:

Q: What do you call a blonde with their hair dyed brown?
A: Artificial intelligence.

This is 100% a blonde joke. Taking the "blonde" out of this one destroys it, because you can't wash the hair color part out - the punchline is the assumption that a person with blonde hair dyeing their hair to another color would temporarily change their intelligence level. Other natural hair colors have other stereotypes connected to them; some ethnicities don't naturally grow blonde hair so they can't be used.

This is the sort of thing we are looking for, only in our case it's looking for outdated topics.

It Can't Be Recycled for a Different Topic or Era

The joke's topic can't be reused in other forms easily. This differs from the previous section "It would fall apart without the outdated topic" which was simply narrowing them by topic. This narrows down by reusability.

Here's a dark humor historical quip that I love:

But other than that, Mrs. Lincoln, how was the play?

President Abraham Lincoln was assassinated in 1865 while watching the play *Our American Cousin*, and his wife was sitting right next to him. The humor here is the idea of brushing off the traumatizing experience of her husband's death and instead asking how the play was – as if she cared about the play after that! I was going to put that joke in here, until in my research I came across:

But other than that, Mrs. Kennedy, how was Dallas?

President John F. Kennedy was assassinated in Dallas, Texas in 1963 while riding in an open car, and his wife was sitting right next to him. It's the same joke, with different characters and setting. Putting it in once would question why the other wasn't put in. Putting in both would double up on jokes, padding the book.

This "no recycled jokes" rule took out a lot of reused humor about events, such as war. War jokes are easily rewritten for the next war. I couldn't find a single, actual this-is-only-about-the-Korean-War joke using my criteria. Oh, I found tons of humor regarding the Korean War, however they were all recycled from previous wars. The American Civil War only has a few in here, none of which were found in the two "American Civil War Humor" books I read.

Unless a reused joke itself becomes outdated - there's one under "automobiles" - I'm not putting it in.

Avoid Puns Unless They Are Very Funny or Apt

I love puns as much as everyone, but they're easy to mass produce and pad up many humor books. Humor books for children are mostly puns, because they're easy to understand for an aspiring humorist and don't have to deal with sarcasm, ridicule, sex, or death — subjects which many children can't handle yet. People often call puns and wordplay "dad jokes" now, but when I was a kid, they were called "groaners," because they often elicit a groan from your audience.

This sort of humor is super easy to make up. Here, I'll make up a "historical pun joke" right now:

> *Q: Did you hear Elvis Presley was in a car accident?*
> *A: He was all shook up.*

Elvis was a very famous entertainer of the mid-20th century, and "All Shook Up" was a number one hit for him in 1957. I'm certainly not the first person to come up with this joke, and I won't be the last.

Why wouldn't I allow this one in here?

Because Elvis was never in any sort of major car accident. He might have been, but it's not really a defining factor of his story of singing, acting, military service, and dying of a drug overdose on the toilet.

I could fill pages and pages with puns on song titles he did, many of which would probably have nothing to do with Elvis himself, and then do the same with hundreds of famous musicians. You can do that on your own, you don't need my help.

Most puns included here tend to be specific to something with historical merit, or a song title most people these days don't know because it's so very far out of the current pop standards, or it's the setup that requires the outdated topic for the pun's payoff.

Nothing After the Year 1999

I will never forget my oldest daughter coming home from school one day around 2010 or so and telling me this joke:

> *Q: How do you get Lady Gaga's attention?*
> *A: Puh-puh-puh poke-her face.*

Okay, boomers (and far-future readers): "Poker Face" was a 2008 hit for Lady Gaga.

I was in shock— for the first time my child had brought home a pop culture quip I had not heard before and dealt specifically with her own generation. I was very proud.

But that one isn't included here, except of course as the above example of what is not included.

What is history? I'm writing this in 2025 and decided to stop in the year 1999. People are still creating humor about events and culture. I know lots of jokes about things that have happened since then, but you must stop somewhere, or people start to get picky about history vs current events.

No humor referring to events after the year 1999 are included. There are some nudges and references, but I still had to draw a line somewhere. More recent technology is still being worked on, the current culture is still with us, the events are still fresh, and people deserve to mourn the sad ones before having the jokes published in books. The humor is already out there, though… you can go look for yourself.

No Censorship

There are lots of great clean jokes in here, but "outdated historical jokes" is the topic, not "clean, fun ones you can tell your children or your moral friends." If a dirty or gross joke has a little historical or topical merit, in it goes.

As I pointed out in the author's note at the beginning, there is probably something here that will offend everyone or at least make them a little uncomfortable. There's also swearing ahead. Again, history isn't always pretty!

Some jokes in this book – particularly about events – can cut a little deep about their subjects. My intention is not to ridicule people or events, but simply to share the forgotten humor related to the subject.

In my own sense of humor there is no such thing as "too soon" when it comes to an event I am not personally invested in, but I still maintain respect for those who are still personally invested in it. Some of the later events listed in this book are from the late 20th century. Some of the people involved are still alive, and their children are still around for sure. That makes me a little uneasy - if they read this book and it brings up some bad memories. I'm not an unfeeling bully. But the jokes were based on public, newsworthy events, I didn't make them up, and they are included for posterity— not to ridicule. Even if the joke takes a side, I personally do not – I'm just a messenger.

Results

I found about 600 jokes that met my criteria.

This made me happy – when I started out with this idea, long before ever putting pen to paper, I wondered if I'd find enough jokes to fill a few pages, let alone a book. Hooray!

However a few jokes were longer than they needed to be. A couple had several different versions, and I needed to choose one. Some actually required translation – even though they were already in English. Some had stereotypes as an artifact of their time that weren't important for the punchline to work. Then, they still needed to be set up and explained.

My job was far from done...

Changes to the Jokes

I got under the hood and did some work on these jokes for clarity. I tidied them up, shortened them, and explained them. I use the term "tidy" here because if I say "cleaning up jokes" people might think I'm taking out the naughty parts of dirty stories.

There was a lot of fluff to be removed and fat to be trimmed. Anyone who picks up this book will find the jokes here in clear English and shortened as much as possible, so any humorist from any background can enjoy them.

Shortening Jokes

I've tried to boil these down as much as possible to only include what is necessary for the punchline. A part of spoken word joke telling is to make it your own by adding some flair to make the story interesting and fun. I trimmed a little of that excess material to focus on the barebones setup and punchline when needed.

Some of the jokes here are feghoots.[1] A feghoot is when you tell a very long story, setting up an amusing pun at the end. These are told in many different and creative ways which can end in the same punchline. I have compressed them as much as possible to preserve the set up and punchline, while keeping the story flow.

---

[1] Feghoots are named after the series of science fiction stories "Through Time and Space with Ferdinand Feghoot" (published 1950s-1970s), which always ended on a pun that was based on a well-known saying.

I give just one version, but if you heard it or told it differently, that's still correct.

Clear English

The humor here is translated into clear early 21st Century English for clarity of understanding.

Some of these jokes were written by people who grew up in the 1800s. Their expressions do differ from current speech to varying degrees.

Proper grammar and English are important to me. As an American, however, a lot of the English here will fall to American English. English, like other languages, is currently in the process of consolidating back from its worldwide variants into…whatever English is turning into. This is a result of the internet because we're not living on isolated continents anymore – we're all communicating, watching each other's TV shows, etc.

Many of these jokes were originally written in language a little archaic even for the version of English it was written in. In updating to today I have a rough time figuring out if we're all going to settle on terms like "elevator or lift," or "petrol or gas," when I update these jokes.

I hope you Brits, Aussies, Kiwis, etc. find this explanation "honourable" enough.

That brings us to….

No Written Dialect

Written dialects have been changed to clear English when the accents aren't required for the punchline.

Many of the jokes included here were published using "eye dialect," to illustrate the vernacular (the language used) of what was considered a lower class of people.

Here's an example from a 1922 joke book, shown here exactly as it was in the book I got it from and then in the clear English version:

<u>In Eye Dialect:</u>

Rastus had caught Sambo red-handed.

"Ah'm gwine hab yo' arrestedfoh stealin' mah chickens, yo' Sambo Washin'ton-dat's jess what ah'm gwine to do," said Rastus.

"Go ahead, nigguh, " retorted Sambo. "Go ahead and hab me arrested. Ah'll mek yo' prove whar yo' got dem chickens yo'seff!"

<u>In Clear English:</u>

Rastus had caught Sambo red-handed.

"I'm going to have you arrested for stealing my chickens; yes, Sambo Washington — that's just what I'm going to do," said Rastus.

"Go ahead, nigger," retorted Sambo. "Go ahead and have me arrested. I'll make you prove where you got those chickens yourself!"

Changing the written word to clear English in no way harms the punchline that Sambo stole Rastus's chickens, which he had already in turn stolen from someone else.

Writing that accent out in a sentence makes things confusing for some readers because there's no standard for writing things out phonetically. Some readers would have to struggle through translating each word, then having to grasp the meaning of each sentence, and then having to figure out the punchline. That's a lot of work!

I'm not saying these "eye dialects" are bad— I remove them more for clarity than to be politically correct. The past was still the past. You can still tell the joke with the dialect— it's easy to identify who these sorts of characters are.

Now that we have an example of a dialect that can be safely removed, here's an example of a joke where the dialect would be important to the punchline:

> *An Irish woman is teaching her daughter how to make a bean stew and said to add only 239 beans to the stew.*
>
> *When the daughter asked why, the mother said [Irish accent] "One mahr bean and 'twould be too-fahrty"*

Doing the math, 239 + 1= 240 "two-forty", and when spoken with an Irish dialect "two forty" and "too farty" rhyme. If you say that with a Midwestern American dialect (like mine) "One more bean and it would be two fohr-tee," then the punchline is lost, or at least would be a wild stretch for the listener.

Generic Stereotype Terms

Humor often relies on a stereotypically stupid character doing something stupid. This trope is the keystone to many, many jokes.

If there is anything humanity has learned from the smaller world brought on by better communication and easier travel, it's that no specific gender, ethnicity, or race makes a person "stupid." All of those groups have their share of intelligent and unintelligent people. Every one of the groups also has people who love humor, and they deserve to read about it without their own group being the butt of every single joke.

Carefully writing around this "stupid character" issue is not new territory for joke books. Pick up any children's joke book and you'll find pages of humor you probably first heard as a stereotype, but instead the character is named the most inoffensive term the author can muster which won't get angry responses from parents, such as "moron" or "doofus."

Because of this, any joke character's ethnicity or race is usually taken out unless it's an important part of the punchline[1] or it would take a lot to rewrite without it.

If the joke requires a "dumb person" role, I have [dumb person] as a placeholder.[2] When you see that, you are welcome to put in any fitting stereotype you want. I'm not offended by whatever group you choose, even if you use

---

[1] Such as the "too farty" joke on page 28

[2] Such as the "How do you get a one armed [dumb person] out of a tree" joke on page 17.

"middle-aged white collector of stale jokes writing a book no one's probably going to want to read."

I try to use neutral genders, but this isn't easy to do in the English language. As a result, I don't watch this as closely with men/women stereotypes as with the other stereotypes. Always consider any story's genders to be swappable <u>if</u> you think it can work. Where there's two people talking, and there's nothing in the joke that requires gender, I say "person" so you can fill in whatever people you want.

Setting Up Background

The following quote is from the comedian Buddy Lester. In it, he is complaining about the satirical comic Mort Sahl, who was becoming famous for his approach of more intelligent, political humor instead of the standard easily-understood fare:

> Who wants a comic you gotta have a dictionary on your lap so you can figure out what he's saying, and even then, he ain't funny!

Well… I've collected jokes you need to have a history book in your lap to understand, and even then, the punchline might not be funny.

These jokes are outdated, and as a result require setup for the casual reader. Sure, *you* may have known that the Dardanelles are a waterway in Turkey that a World War I naval battle was fought over (good for you!), but many people don't (I sure didn't), and I'm trying to keep that in mind.

I try to give just enough historical info for the punchline to be understood. And yes, sometimes that means the setup will be far longer than the joke itself. *Remember:* this is the reason that joke is in this book of outdated humor! I'm not giving you a full history, but I'm giving you enough to do your own research if the event is something you were unfamiliar with and now interests you.

The contents of the actual joke, however, are a story and usually depend on some suspension of disbelief. Humor has a lot in common with folklore, in that they're both oral stories passed down from person to person and endlessly edited to fit the audience for amusement. Jokes are fiction. They take place in a different world, similar to ours, but working by different rules in service to the punchline. They sometimes don't stand up well to logic and reason— but neither do most books and movies in the end.

Jokes about real events are usually made up by people who weren't there and heard about them second hand. They may have some aspects of the event completely wrong or have preconceived notions about the topic long before an official investigation found the truth.

Always beware when assuming that something is true just because you heard it in a joke.

Explaining Punchlines

It is said that explaining a joke is like dissecting a frog. Sure, you understand the frog better, but the frog is dead.

Well, I'm explaining them. The jokes are dead anyway; we've exhumed them, so why not perform an autopsy while we're at it? Or maybe we're bringing them back from the dead as zombies! We're like Doctor Frankenstein, giving life to the monster! And they called me mad! MAD! MWAH-HA-HA!

...Ahem. Sorry. Got a little carried away there.

This will sometimes include explaining jokes where the punchline should be very obvious, even to a [dumb person]. I apologize if you roll your eyes at the explanation, however I do not know what every individual reader will get or not.

We've all come across humor here and there which we didn't "get." It really bugs me when I never figure it out, even after asking other people their opinion. Sometimes I even want to ask the author of the book "what's this one about?" because I'm utterly stumped. The fact is many authors are more interested in declaring there are thousands of jokes in their books for better sales than to stop and check if each and every one actually makes sense.

Because I'm explaining the jokes, I can assure you that every bit of humor here is an actual joke with a punchline I can point out and explain. If I didn't get it, I didn't put it in— except in a few cases here and there, and I'll talk about it when that happens.

I respect that part of the fun for some folks is treating the joke like a puzzle to be solved. That's fine - you can skip the explanations if that's your thing. However we're all getting participation trophies here. Yay!

Mind you, I'm only giving you one punchline. Some jokes can have multiple punchlines. If you think "Wait, it's funny because of this thing he didn't mention!" you're still right!

Categories

This book is in three broad categories: technology, events, and culture.

- **Technology** covers now-obsolete technology, or the early days of a current technology. The technology section is split into three categories:
    - *Communication*
    - *Appliances and Devices*
    - *Travel*
- **Events** goes down the timeline, mentioning events and happenings as they occurred.
    - The Events section is in chronological order, roughly 1800s to 1999.
- **Culture** covers events and things that can't really be tied to a specific date. Products come and go, services that you can still get but aren't done the same way. I try to give you a time frame when I can.
    - You could also call this section "everything else."

There's not an entry for every topic you'd like

In the process of writing this book, I looked over outlines of the 19th and 20th centuries, and for each major event I went searching for humor pertaining to them, following my own rules. Often, I found more jokes of one type than another, or I found nothing.

I freely acknowledge that under "movies" in this book there's a single joke about normal, sit-down movie theaters and then the rest of the jokes are about drive-in movie theaters, which are a bygone thing today. This sort of imbalance of jokes annoys me, but I had to work with what I found.

This issue is common in joke books. A 1922 toasting anecdote book I read only had one or two entries for some of the topics I expected there to be lots of entries for - common human things such as:

Reputation: 2 entries
Pride: 2 entries
Carelessness: 1 entry
Wealth: 1 entry
Chicken stealing: ...8 entries?

I'm amused by the idea of a world where a speaker at a fancy formal dinner is more likely to crack a joke about chicken stealing than about reputation or wealth!

Again, I'm the messenger, not the creator. I was limited by what I could find, so if you are left sitting there wondering, "Why are there none about this?" or "Why are there none about that?" trust me, I wish there were! But there's not... or I just haven't found them yet.

Okay, that's enough yapping. Let's get on with the jokes!

Technology: Communication

Newspapers

Newspapers were once the primary source of news among people who could read.

This is an 1860s joke from one newspaper about another. It involves the newspaper presses being animal or steam operated, playing off an "ass" being a term for both a donkey, and an idiot.

> *Some newspaper establishments are operated by steam. In others, horse or ass power is employed.*
>
> *Should our neighbor obtain, as he promises, a steam press, he will have a combination of advantages— a paper printed by steam and edited by an ass.*

Newspapers would be delivered to your home by a paperboy, who would also be the person that collected the money for it. This pokes fun at how paperboys were sometimes reliable, sometimes not.

> *A paperboy is someone who shows up once a week to collect for the daily paper he had delivered once a week.*

This is a play on being physically tired, and tired of the news.

A man saw a paperboy carrying a load of newspapers under his arm and inquired if they made him tired.

"No," the paperboy responded, "I don't read them."

Here's a crafty paperboy:

Newsboy: Great mystery! Fifty victims! Paper, mister?
Passerby: I'll take one. [reads a moment] Say, boy— there's nothing of the kind in this paper. Where is it?
Newsboy: That's the mystery, sir. You're the fifty-first victim.

People would steal newspapers off doorsteps. There were coin-operated kiosks that couldn't dispense just one paper; it would open revealing a stack of newspapers and you were supposed to take one on the honor system, but many people would take several.

"I don't get the newspaper anymore because my neighbor just moved. When I do buy the paper, I buy them out of the coin racks: they're cheaper. They're four for a quarter out of those things." [1]

[1] Gary Shandling

The speaker is joking about his being cheap. They were stealing their neighbor's newspaper and grabbing extras out of the "coin rack" kiosks.

The Army saves you a fortune in newspapers. If there's trouble anywhere in the world, they send you right over. You don't have to read about it!

The above joke implies you don't have to spend money to find out if there was a war anywhere or what was going on in it because you were already there.

Sunday papers tended to be the largest edition of the week. They'd be full of articles, a color comics section, and coupons. This took advantage of the fact that families stayed home on Sunday, as it was a day to go to church and to rest for most people, though this culture faded after the 1950s.

This is a joke about the size of the Sunday edition:

The nice part about reading the Sunday Times from beginning to end is that there's only three hours left until the Monday edition comes out.

And this is about the Sunday comics "funny paper" section. The boy isn't as pure and sweet as the nanny thinks. A "nursemaid" is an in-house person/servant who looks after small children.

Albert was a quiet, spiritual-looking child. "Nurse," he quietly asked his new nursemaid, "is this God's Day?"

"No dear, this is not Sunday, it's Thursday."

The next day and the next Albert did this, and the nurse thought to herself about what a sweet, pure child he was, obviously too good and holy for this rough world.

On Sunday the question was asked again and the nurse happily replied "Yes, Albert, this is God's Day."

"THEN WHERE IS THE FUNNY PAPER?" Albert demanded.

After people were finished reading their newspaper, the paper would be reused for various odd jobs around the house, such as wrapping meat, wrapping gifts, papier mache crafts, or putting them down for pets to do their business on when inside. The following joke is a reference to how you can't use a radio for these purposes. This joke was later reused with "television" replacing the word "radio."

They used to believe that radio would replace the newspaper, but it never happened. You can't housebreak a dog on a radio.

It points out you can't spread out the radio on the floor for the dog to poop on, like you can a newspaper.

This uses the term "papers" double meaning here being a show dog's pedigree and housebreaking a dog.

> *Of course my dog has papers! We spread them out on the floor for him!*

And...

> *Young Adult: Dad, where's yesterday's newspaper?*
> *Father: Your mother wrapped the garbage in it and threw it away.*
> *Young Adult: Darn, I wanted to see it.*
> *Father: There wasn't much to see, just some old egg cartons, dog food cans, and apple cores.*

The father was saying what they had been missing regarding the garbage, and not the news.

Small-town newspapers were written only for the specific small town's residents. If you ever dig into back issues of small-town newspapers, you'll see that they weren't intended to be read by people outside of town. You find the writers referring to the town as "this place", assuming the readers are familiar with where they are. They'll also refer to specific locals as if the reader already knows them and even listing the home addresses of the people they are talking about, which today would be viewed as an invasion of privacy.

A small town is a place where everybody knows what everyone else is doing but they read the local paper to see if their neighbors have been caught at it.

Early photographs were expensive to take, develop and print, so small town newspapers covering a local wedding or lavish party would use excessive detail describing how the people were dressed. That's the background for the joke here:

Fed up with the fancy descriptions he had to set in type day after day, a printer on the Mena, Arkansas Star added this on his own to the end of a wedding story:

"The linotype[1] operator, while he set this, wore a pale blue shirt with pants to match and a silver wristwatch on his left wrist."

In the era of smartphones most people can find out the current date in a moment or ask someone who does. This joke depends on checking a newspaper for that.

First Person: What's the date today?
Second Person: Why don't you look at that newspaper you're holding?

---

[1] A linotype "line-o-type" machine was a revolutionary typesetting machine aiding in publishing for almost a hundred years before computers took over. It could produce an entire line of metal type at once, hence the name.

First Person: It won't do any good - it's yesterday's paper.

If the first person knows it's yesterday's paper, then some simple math would tell them today's date.

With the decline of newspapers, it's worth mentioning an old kids' joke standard:

Q: What's black and white and red all over?
A: A newspaper.

It's a riddle playing off the pun of "red" being a color and the past tense of reading: "read." The joke isn't very funny itself except as a riddle, but a lot of fun has been had with alternate answers that fit the description such as a chocolate sundae with ketchup on it, a skunk in a blender, or a nun falling down a hill.

What makes the joke a little dated is that physical newspapers aren't as "read all over" as they once were, when there was a kiosk on every corner, and a copy on everyone's doorstep each morning.

Encyclopedias

Encyclopedias were with us and republished regularly for many years, a household repository of knowledge in a set of volumes on your bookshelf, before the internet and Wikipedia took over.

The following is a humorous classified newspaper ad about a person getting rid of an encyclopedia because the seller has upgraded:

> *For sale by owner: complete set of Encyclopedia Brittanica. 45 Volumes, $1,000 or best offer. Got married, wife knows everything.*

This next one fakes the listener out by upsetting the expected "learning" by the fact that they had hidden money in their encyclopedia.

> *I once went through the Encyclopedia, and it really taught me something: never hide a five-dollar bill without remembering the page number!*

On the spine - the narrow side of the book that holds the pages together - of each volume of an encyclopedia, there would be the first few letters of the first entry for that volume, followed by the first few letters of the last entry. This assisted people in finding the volume for the topic they wanted alphabetically, which leads to the following joke.

> *A [dumb person] tried to check a book out of the library called "How to Hug," but the librarian explained that reference books like the encyclopedia can't be checked out.*

The person thought it was a book on how to hug someone, when the above fictional volume was the entries [from] HOW to HUG.

Nelson's Encyclopaedia was published from 1906 to 1934. Its gimmick was offering loose-leaf, removable pages so you could buy individual new pages to update your encyclopedia without having to buy new volume versions or a whole new set.

> *Salesman: Are you interested in a loose-leaf encyclopedia?*
> *Man: Nope, got one.*
> *Salesman: Indeed! Whose?*
> *Man: The Britannica.*
> *Salesman: I didn't know they published a loose-leaf edition.*
> *Man: Huh! You ought to see mine after the children have used the volumes as building blocks for a few years.*

The children used the volumes for building blocks, eventually breaking the spines of the volumes and making the pages fall out.

The Telegraph and Telegrams

The telegraph took off in the middle of the 1800s, allowing near-instant transmission of information between places. You would pay per word, send the telegram, and for an extra fee could have the printed telegram delivered directly to the person.

Today we have texting and messaging on smartphones but imagine if to send a text you had to leave your home and go to a storefront in town, give your text message to a complete stranger who would then read it and send it. You would pay for the service immediately or ask for the receiving person to pay the fee before they could be handed the message. That's the telegraph.[1]

Telegraphs required long wires strung between places on poles, which though common today were pretty new for the time.

> *Soon after the installation of a telegraph to town, a little boy noticed that a piece of newspaper had blown onto the telegraph wire and caught on it.*
>
> *He ran to his mother and exclaimed "Come quick! The telegraph wire busted and is letting all the news out!"*

The boy imagined the information went down the wire like water through a pipe and was leaking out in the form of a newspaper.

Here you are going to have to stretch your suspension of disbelief that they found wires under an old castle for the payoff of "not finding wires" under a castle proving there was wireless telegraphy.

> *An Irishman and a Scot were arguing as to the merits of their respective countries. "Ah well," said Sandy, "they tore down an old castle in Scotland and found many wires*

[1] Text messages were never on a pay-per-word basis, but they were pay-per-message until unlimited texting plans became common, around 2010.

under it, which shows that the telegraph was known in Scotland hundreds of years ago."

"Well," said Pat, "They tore down an old castle in Ireland, and found no wires under it, which shows that they knew all about wireless telegraphy in Ireland hundreds of years ago."

I've seen this joke used several times, each time having different cultures, countries, or states but the punchline of "Didn't find wires so they had wireless first" is the same.

Telegrams were filled out and given to a telegrapher, who sent the message to its destination over the wires using Morse code. At the other end it was deciphered and typed up, then sent to the recipient.

A telegraph operator lives on tick.

"Tick" here being a double meaning - the "tick" sound of the telegraph sending/receiving noise and "tick" short for "ticket," slang for debt or credit.

The character in the next joke does not understand the telegraph process, assuming that it is much like writing a letter:

A woman stopped in a telegraph office to send a message to her son but had difficulty figuring out how to fill out the telegraph form. Thinking the woman was illiterate, the clerk offered to write in the message for her at her dictation.

"That wouldn't work," she replied, "My son wouldn't recognize your handwriting."

This next gentleman doesn't understand that the message has to be read by the operator before it can be sent over the wire:

A man was in court for assault.
"Why did you strike the telegraph operator?" asked the judge.
"Well, sir, I gave him a telegram to send to my girl, and he started reading it. So of course I punched him!"

Telegrams were paid for on a per-word basis. The fewer words, the cheaper the telegram fee.

In the next joke, the telegram was sent COD (Cash On Delivery), where the receiver would pay when they got it.

Telegram delivery person: Here's a telegram from a friend for you. That will be ten dollars.
Customer: Ten dollars? That can't be. I don't have any friends who know ten dollars' worth of words.

He's making a joke that his friends have a limited vocabulary, so they couldn't possibly send him such an expensive telegram.

Then, there's this:

> *A group of friends went on a picnic, but their friend Anna sat on a fire ant hill, and she got bitten badly enough to require hospitalization. Anna's parents needed to be informed, and long-distance phone calls were pretty expensive, especially for college students. They decided to send a telegram. They pooled what spare money they had and trooped down to the telegraph office. They asked how many words they could send for the money they had, and were told, "Six."*
>
> *After some head scratching, they sent: "Anacin hospital adamant bitter asinine places."*

The humor above is in that the mix of seemingly unrelated words sounds like "Anna's in hospital, a damn ant bit her ass in nine places."

There was no fee for including the name of the telegram sender, because you had to know who it was from. This lead to jokes about exploiting this.

> *A boyfriend signed "Xerxes" on all his telegrams to his girl so he could get in two kisses without paying for them.*

Often in letters "hugs and kisses" is abbreviated with "X's and O's" They got two kisses: "X's" in free by putting them in his "name."

The man started to write a telegram for his wife, when the person at the desk told him there was no charge for his name.

Putting down his pencil, the man said, "I may not look like one, but I am a [foreigner], and my name is "Iwontbehometillsaturdaynight."

He was trying to save money by having his "name" be part of the message: "I won't be home until Saturday night." As for the [foreigner] part I added, the joke used "Indian,"[1] change it as you'd like, but pick a culture with complicated-sounding names.

The above joke was later the basis of a popular Geico insurance television commercial in the late 1990s, having the telephone caller tell the operator they wanted to place a collect call (the recipient pays the charges, not the caller) from "Bob Wehadababyitsaboy" ("We had a baby, it's a boy"), and the call recipient refused the charges because it was "the wrong number"... then hung up and immediately told his wife about Bob's new baby. [2]

You can still hire companies to do a "singing telegram" for fun, but getting a normal telegram is rare today. Here's a joke about mixing the two, and why that might not be a good idea:

---

[1] The joke didn't clarify if they meant a Native American or a person from India.

[2] While insurance has little to do with placing collect calls, the final tagline of the commercial was "Don't cheat the phone company, save money the legal way. Call Geico."

A man answers the door to find a telegraph delivery guy, who says "Telegram for you, sir."

The man says "You know what? I've never had a singing telegram before. I'll pay you $25 to sing that telegram for me."

The delivery person looks uncomfortable, but the guy persists. "...tell you what. $50 to sing it for me - no, make it $100!"

The delivery person considers this, looks down at the telegram and sings, "Your mother is dead!"

The following is a joke about how telegraph rates were cheaper off-peak hours:

A boy went to the telegraph office with his father and listened to his father's conversation with the clerk. That evening he asked his mother what prayers were. She said that prayers were "messages to God."

He said, "Well, do we pray to him at bedtime because the night rates are cheaper?"

This is a penny-pinching man who tests and finds his dream girl.

A man telegraphed a proposal of marriage to the girl he loved. After waiting all day at the telegraph office for a reply, her "yes" came late at night.

"Well, if I were you," said the telegraph operator, "I'd think twice before I married the girl who kept me waiting for an answer so long."

"No, no!" replied the man. "The girl for me is one who waits for night rates!"

Western Union, the biggest delivery and telegram service, had a slogan about how if you need a messenger boy to deliver something, you should call them. The joke here is the double-meaning when the slogan is paired with the telegram.

A man away on business waited eagerly for news of his wife delivering their first child. Finally, the telegram arrived "Your wife gave birth to a little girl this morning: both doing well."

On the message was a sticker saying "If you want a boy, call Western Union"

Telegrams were fast, and the following joke is that the wife was able to land at her destination and then send a telegram which beat him home on his drive across New York City. The stated route implies two busy bridges and Manhattan traffic.

A Brooklyn gentleman took his wife to Newark, New Jersey airport and put her on a plane to Buffalo, New York.

After fighting his way through traffic, he arrived home and wearily ascended the steps to his front door, finding a telegram already in the mailbox "Arrived safely. Love, Lulu."

Telegrams took a few extra steps, so this sort of thing was very unlikely but still possible back in those days. What's interesting today is that you can get a text from someone you dropped off at the airport the moment their airplane's wheels touch the runway at their destination, depending on how fast they got through security before takeoff and the length of their flight, and considering if you got stuck in traffic or ran errands on the way home.

Photography

Today most photography is done electronically and instantly. It used to be that a camera exposed the light onto a chemical film which had to be developed professionally. The film would create "negatives" where lightest areas of the picture were darkest, and the darkest areas were lightest because of how the physical camera took the picture by letting light in. Developing the images involved applying chemicals to the negatives and enlarging the result.

Early cameras needed a lot of light – not all at once, but over time. As a result the subjects needed to sit very still for a minute or so. This was understandably rough on children. There's a very funny two-panel cartoon in *Punch's Almanack* for 1855 showing a nice family sitting for a daguerreotype (early photograph), and in the second panel the "result" is a mess with the family members unrecognizable because they were moving around while the picture was taken.

Photographic plates and film have to be developed in as little light as possible, giving the name to the literal "darkroom". This was to not affect the images before they were completely developed into the prints, which are the final photographs.

Here's a photography joke about how "seemingly difficult girls are easy to get into bed"

> *Many girls with a negative personality may be developed in a dark room.*

And this is about how you had to wait to get your pictures developed after taking them:

> *First Person: I have a photographic memory.*
> *Second Person: So why do you forget so many things?*
> *First Person: Is it my fault it hasn't developed yet?*

The "developed" joke is used again here, meaning "we'll see what happens."

Patient: Doctor, I think I swallowed a roll of film!
Doctor: Relax. We'll wait and see what develops.

This one uses a pun: "prints" (photographs) for "prince," and the song Snow White sings at the beginning of the 1937 movie *Snow White and the Seven Dwarfs*.

Q: What did Snow White sing when she dropped off her film at the developer?
A: "Someday my prints will come."

The actual song is "Someday my *Prince* will Come."

Niece: Auntie, have you got your photographs yet?"
Auntie: Yes, and I sent them back in disgust."
Niece: Gracious! What was wrong?
Auntie: On the back of every photo was written: 'The original of this is carefully preserved.' "

The meaning of the message on the back of the photo is that there is an original print preserved by the photographer to make more prints from in case those are lost. Auntie assumed the photographer was referring to herself as "the original which has been carefully preserved" - she thinks the photographer is calling her "old."

Some photographers had toy birds to signal which direction the subject should face for the portrait. "Smile for the birdie" was the same as "say cheese" in the era but had the added bonus of keeping the person looking in one direction so they didn't move around during the picture.

This next joke is proof that the "child who is knowledgeable about new technology" that we see with technology today is truly timeless:

> *Photographer: Please smile for the little birdie.*
>
> *Youngster: Oh, drop that "little birdie" stuff! Get out your light meter and do some tests, adjust your lighting properly, and set your lens correctly so you won't ruin a sensitized plate!*

People couldn't see the pictures until after they were developed by a store, which was often weeks or even months later. They also didn't want to waste the untaken pictures on the roll so people would take some random pictures of things or people just to finish the roll off and get their money's worth.

> *"My family is really boring. They have a coffee table book called "Pictures We Took Just to Use Up the Rest of the Film"* [1]

There's an urban legend that requires waiting for the development of film for its twist.

---

[1] Penelope Lombard

A couple returned to their hotel room to find that they had been robbed. All their luggage and property had been taken except, oddly enough, their camera and their toothbrushes. They were able to get new things and enjoy the rest of their vacation. They joked about how they were still able to take pictures and brush their teeth and even took some pictures of themselves brushing their teeth with the toothbrushes.

When they got the developed film back, they both gagged when they saw one picture that they themselves hadn't taken was of a man's bare bottom, cheeks spread ...with both of their toothbrushes stuck up inside it.

Radio

In the late 1800s to early 1900s, radio was simply a telegraph without wires, sending Morse code over the air. It took some work before they could broadcast speech and sound over the radio.

Son: Dad, what's the difference between telegraph and radio?

Dad: Well son, imagine a dog so long that if you step on its tail in New York, it barks in Chicago. That's telegraph. Radio is the same thing, but without the dog.

That joke is also told with "…but the dog is invisible."

Radio signals were called "airwaves," as in "Waves coming through the air." Playing your radio too loudly led to obvious noise complaints. This links radio to airplanes, which was also a new technology at the time.

> *Man has conquered the air but so has our neighbor's radio.*

Early radio stations didn't pre-record anything; it was all live.[1] The stations would shut down and stop broadcasting for the night and then start again in the morning. You can imagine people might fall asleep listening to the radio, just like today with television and internet videos. As a result they would never turn their radio off for the evening, which leads to this joke:

> *Radio announcers should start off the morning broadcast by yelling "Who the hell left the radio on all night?"*

Today radio still has advertisements, however in the early days of radio these ads were read live on the air by the announcer. As mentioned previously nothing was recorded ahead of time. This was a new thing for people because in newspapers you could simply ignore

---

[1] I assume everyone understands what I mean by "live", but to use modern online terminology for an old technology, everything in the early days of radio and television was "live streamed", the now-common term originating in the 1990s.

advertisements on the page, but now you had to sit through them.

> *A radio announcer is a man who tries to get a commercial in before the listener can change stations.*

The station you wanted to listen to sometimes had to be fine-tuned with a physical knob you turned, and an issue with radio before digital tuners was getting just the right spot on your radio dial to listen to the station you wanted and not another.[1] Signals bounced off things like buildings and hills as they made their way from the station antenna to your radio receiver, leading to some mixing of stations near each other on the dial. Getting two stations playing at the same time was possible and is the basis for this joke:

> *A man's wife asked him to copy a recipe off the radio. He did his best but got two stations at once. This is what he wrote down:*
>
> *Hands on hips; place 1 cup of flour on your shoulder; raise knees and depress toes; mix thoroughly in 1/2 cup of milk; repeat six times, inhale quickly; 1/2 teaspoon of baking powder; lower the legs and mash 2 hard-boiled eggs in a sieve; exhale breath naturally and sift in a bowl; Attention! Lie flat on the floor and roll in the whites of two*

---

[1] Just like how hard it is to set a shower control to just the right spot for not too hot, and not too cold.

> *eggs backward and forward until it comes to a boil; In 10 minutes remove from fire and rub smartly with a rough towel; breathe naturally, dress in warm flannels and serve with tomato soup.*

The radio soap opera *The Guiding Light* (1937-1952)[1] used live organ music for its opening and closing, which was quickly adopted by other radio soap operas.

> *They say soap operas are true to life, but that's ridiculous. When did you ever have a 30-minute argument with your wife that ended in organ music?*

Movies

Movies, also called "cinema," "moving pictures," and "flicks," really took off in the between 1910 and 1920. This was before television, so you had to go to a theater to see this new technology.

> *An old couple from the country wandered into a moving picture show in town. As they entered a cowboy picture was being shown. The old lady laid a restraining hand on her husband's arm.*
>
> *"Bill," she said, "let's not go too far down the front; the dust those horses are*

[1] Guiding Light moved to television in 1952 and ran until 2009.

> *kicking up is something awful. My clothes will be ruined!"*

The woman thought there would be real dust kicked up by the horses.

The heyday of drive-in theaters, where you could park your car and watch a movie, was from the 1930s to the 1970s.

> *Wanted: Bouncer for drive-in movie theater. Must have own tow truck.*

The joke is you'd need a tow truck to remove unruly people from a drive-in because they were in a car.

Of course, many young people were more interested in being alone together in a car than watching a movie.

> *There's nothing more interesting than seeing a murder mystery at a drive-in movie theater, because after the movie is over no one knows who did it!*

And…

> *There are three different kinds of people who go to drive in movies. Those who watch the movie, those who don't watch the movie, and those who keep adjusting their rear-view mirrors.*

Adjusting their mirrors to spy on couples making out.

Drive-in movie theaters could make a little money on Sunday mornings by letting a church have services there:

> *I don't mind going to church services at a drive-in theater, but when they hold baptisms in a car wash it's gone too far.*

The Christian rite of baptism involves sprinkling holy water on someone or full-body immersion in it.

No one wanted to sit in a cold car watching a movie, so winter would put a stop on drive-ins each year.

> *Did you hear about the [dumb person] who went to see a movie at the drive-in called "Closed for the winter, see you in the spring"?*

The theater was closed for the season, and that was the notice on the marquee, taking the place of current movies.

Telephones: The Early Days

Alexander Graham Bell patented the telephone in 1877, and telephones are still with us today. They've gone through many, many changes over the years, each with their own jokes. As you are going to see in the following sections, the experience of using a telephone changed over time.

This next joke assumes if we weren't waiting for a phone to ring, then we'd be waiting for something else in the house to ring. A bridge lamp is a tall reading lamp, but here it could be any other household item.

> *Did you know that if Alexander Graham Bell hadn't invented the telephone, we'd all be sitting around waiting for the bridge lamp to ring?*

The following joke merely makes a funny point:

> *Alexander Graham Bell invented the telephone, but true credit belongs to the person who invented the second telephone.*

...because you need *another telephone to call* from the first. In reality, the "second telephone" wasn't invented, it was built at the same time from the same plans as the first. One telephone by itself is useless, and the humor is from the idea of the inventor building a telephone and then sitting around waiting for someone else to invent one, build it, and call them.

This is from a list of various things with humorous definitions, here defining a telephone:

> <u>*Telephone*</u>*: An invention of the Devil which cancels out some of the advantages of making a disagreeable person keep their distance.*

You used to be able to simply stay away from people you didn't like, however with the invention of the telephone you still had to talk to them even when they weren't physically present.

And of course, there were many jokes which came down to "if you're going to yell into the phone that loudly, you don't really need the phone, do you?"

> *Businessman: Who is the boss yelling at in his office?*
> *Secretary: He's speaking to the San Francisco office.*
> *Businessman: Well, why doesn't he just use the telephone?*

The boss was indeed using the telephone; he was just angry and yelling.

On the flip side of this, people would mumble and whisper into the phone, too.

> *In an uptown [New York] phone booth, someone found this reminder note:*
>
> *1: Tell her you love her.*
> *2: Ask for a date*
> *3: Speak loudly.*

The person in question needed a reminder to project their voice in seeking the heart of the woman over the phone.

Telephones: Telephone Cords

Phone cords, connecting the base to the handset, were coiled to permit the user to stretch the cord giving more freedom of movement. They notoriously ended up with kinks and twists in them.

> *"How does the phone cord get all tangled? All I do is talk and hang up. I don't pick it up and do a cartwheel and a somersault."* [1]

Cordless phones were developed in the late 1970s. These weren't modern-day mobile phones as the range was limited to about 50 feet if you were lucky, but you could walk around your home or even go outside without a cable connecting you to the line. This leads to the following joke which is prophetic for trying to find your mobile phone around the house today:

> *"Cordless phones are great. If you can find them."* [2]

Later cordless phones did introduce a button on the charging station which, when pressed, would make the cordless phone beep so you could find it. Of course, that wasn't any good if the phone was too far away or had lost its charge.

---

[1] Larry Miller

[2] Glenn Foster

Telephones: Telephone Directories

The telephone directory, or "phone book," was a directory of local phone numbers. In large cities these were massive volumes. Many children would be given a phone book to use as a booster seat when at the dinner table.

The following is a heavily-used phone book joke, its humor being from how anyone could actually read the entire phone book and assume it was a work of fiction or intended for entertainment.[1]

I just read a phone book to pass the time.
Lots of characters, but not much of a plot.

Or an extension of the above…

A [dumb person] storms into the library, complaining about the book they had checked out. They say there's no plot, just lots of characters.

The librarian replies, "So you're the one who stole our phone book!"

Or…

---

[1] That's not to say there wasn't some humor buried in there by jokesters. In 1992, while I was still in high school, a friend grabbed my Pittsburgh Metropolitan Area phone book and showed me that someone had their name listed in it as "Zaphod Beeblebrox," a character from the 1970s radio/book series *The Hitchhiker's Guide to the Galaxy.*

I tried to read the phone book, but I got bored during the Ws.

The joke being that the "W" names are really a ridiculously long way to get through the phone book before getting bored.

Q: Why are there so many Johnsons in the phone book?
A: They all have phones!

This is anti-humor. The listener is expecting a funny response, but of course they're in the phone book… because they have telephones.

First Person: Give me your telephone number and I'll call you up sometime.
Second Person: It's in the phone book.
First Person: Fine! What's your name?
Second Person: It's in the phone book, too.

The person either doesn't want to give out their information or simply isn't very bright. Both ideas work for the joke.

Being listed in the phone directory was included in the price of the phone, but if you valued your privacy and did not want to be listed, you had to spend more money to have an unlisted number. This joke plays off unlisted numbers, a ringing phone, and the real condition of tinnitus (a sound in or "ringing" ears).

Patient: Doctor, my ear keeps ringing!
Doctor: Maybe you should get an unlisted ear.

The following more modern jokes play off the fact that in the early 2000s with the rise of the internet, phone books became unwanted practically overnight and are now rarely seen around the house. I include them because they are specifically from the older generation which lived through those early days of phone books and into the internet age.

Beat your kids with a phone book. They won't even know what hit them!

"Didn't know what hit" a person means something that happened so fast the person can't figure out what happened, and here it plays with "not knowing what item hit them."

This one involves the modern smartphone - introduced in 2007 - which came after my self-imposed "cutoff point" of 1999. The existence of both in the same story is possible, but mostly a plot device simply to get to the punchline.

I asked my child for the phone book. They said, "Get with the times! Everyone uses their smartphone now!" and gave me theirs.

Now they are crying because their smartphone is broken, but at least the spider is dead.

The parent wanted the phone book as something heavy to kill a spider, not to look something up.

Telephones: *Party Lines*

A "party line" was a shared phone service. If you picked up your home phone and someone was already using it, you would have to wait for those people to finish before you could contact the operator to call the number you wanted. However, you could also sit and listen in or join in the conversation.

> *First Person: There's a story in this newspaper about a woman who spoke on a telephone for the first time in eighty-three years.*
> *Second Person: She must have been on a party line.*

The above plays off "the person first used a telephone at eighty-three years old" and "the person finally got a break in the conversation to ask to use the phone after waiting eighty-three years."

This next joke involves a party line and makes fun of someone saying they are not there.

> *A man was holding his telephone receiver, and while waiting for a chance to call the operator he heard this conversation on the party line.*
> *First Person: Hello?*
> *Second Person: Hello.*
> *First Person: That you, Jake?*
> *Second Person: Yep, this is Jake.*

First Person: It doesn't sound like Jake.
Second Person: Well, this is Jake speaking, all right.
First Person: Are you sure this is Jake?
Second Person: Sure, this is Jake!
First Person: Well, listen, Jake. This is Henry. Lend me fifty dollars.
Second Person: All right, I'll tell Jake when he comes in.

This person cleverly got a talkative person off the party line.

A young lady picked up the phone and discovered that the party line was in use. "I just put on a pan of beans for dinner," she heard one woman complacently informing another.

She hung up the receiver and waited. Three times she checked and waited, and then, exasperated, she broke into the conversation.

"Madam, I smell your beans burning," she announced crisply. A horrified scream greeted the remark, and the young lady was able to put in her call

Telephones: Operators

Early on, there were no physical dials or buttons on home telephones.[1] When you wanted to call someone, you picked up the earpiece, and it connected you to an operator whom you asked to connect you to the telephone exchange you wanted to speak to. The operators were mostly female, leading to this joke:

> *I didn't realize the phone company had male operators until I got one on the phone. I asked to speak to an operator, and he said, "I am an operator."*
>
> *I said, "Well how do you know you're an operator?"*
>
> *He replied "Well, I'm alone with 85 women."*

An "operator" here means both a phone operator and "A ladies' man."

Operators were humans, too, and couldn't simply be there at the moment you picked up the line.

> *"Has the line been busy?" asked the man who had been waiting to make a call. "No," answered the operator. "The line wasn't busy. I was."*

[1] You know what? Modern smartphones don't have those either!

Telephones: Exchange Names

From the 1930s to the 1960s in the United States, phone numbers went by the exchange name and then a number, such as "BEechwood 4-5789," or "PEnnsylvania 6-5000."[1] Only the first two letters of the word were actually important, but using the word made it easier to remember.

> *Operator: You want HOllywood 1234? The line is busy. But I could give you HOllywood 4321 or GLadstone 1234— they are very nice numbers.*

The operator is offering different numbers, which is just silly.

This uses the exchange name "BLoomfield" in this one, but without mentioning numbers.

> *Telephone Operator: It costs seventy-five cents to talk to BLoomfield.*
> *Caller: Can't you make a special rate for just listening? I want to call my wife.*

No, there were no special rates for just listening on your end.

---

[1] The examples I give here are song titles that reference those early phone numbers: "BEechwood 4-5789" was a 1962 hit for the Marvelettes, and "PEnnsylvania 6-5000" was a 1940 hit for Glen Miller.

The teacher asked the student, "When did Moses live?" and after the silence became painful, he ordered the child, "Open your Old Testament. What does it say there?"

The student answered, "Moses 4000."

"Now," said the teacher, "Why didn't you know when Moses lived?"

"Well," the student replied, "I thought it was his phone number"

That joke isn't very clear on exactly where or how in his Bible the student got "Moses 4000," that part doesn't make much sense, but the mistaking it for a phone number is the punchline.

Telephones: Landlines

Early phones had to be connected to the telephone wires, hence the term "landlines." Most houses only had one phone— extra lines were an added, unnecessary expense.

This joke depends on a shared home telephone.

A child secretly tried his mother's brandy, and soon after used the telephone.

A little later after that the child's father, who was out, called the mother on the phone to inform her that he would be late getting home.

"Yes, and I know why," she replied.

"Ah, how do you know?"

"You're drinking again and intend to be out all night!"

"I am not," protested the father. "I haven't touched a drop for a year."

"Oh, you can't fool me!" insisted his wife, "I can smell it on your breath."

The mother was smelling it on the phone from the child's use before, not from the father's breath.

Of course, chatting teenagers tended to be in line for the telephone:

Every night after dinner I spend what I call "children's hour." I wait for them to get off the phone.

Here's a cute little poem about how the kids going to school would free up the telephone for your own use:

School has begun.
You're feeling alone,
But you haven't lost kids,
What you've gained is a phone!

An actual second phone line is used in this joke:

A father was so tired of his teen son always talking on the phone, he had a second line put in just for the son.

One night the father found his son on the family telephone, and he yelled at him to use his own. The son responded "No way, Dad! One of my friends might call on it!"

Telephones: Etiquette

Early on the rules for etiquette on the phone were still being settled on by society. Remember, this was before caller ID[1] or having contacts on your phone, and you had no idea who or what number was calling your telephone—it simply rang and you picked it up and answered.

Today most people have their own individual phone, their own number. Back then there was often only one phone for the household. Asking a caller to a home phone if they would like to speak to the person the caller is asking for is polite; after all, the caller might just want to pass along a short message for the person they were calling for, such as "No, just tell him…" etc. Still, there was a joking response to this:

Answerer: Hello?
Caller: Hi, is Bob there?
Answerer: Yes, do you wish to speak to him?
Caller [sarcastically] No, I'm just seeing if he's there.

Some people would just start asking who they were speaking to or what number they had dialed before stating

[1] Caller ID was introduced in the 1980's and for a fee you could have a little LED display by your phone showing you what number was calling. There was a charge for the service, so most people didn't have it.

who they were or why they were calling. These are funny responses to that.

Answerer: Hello?
Caller: What number is this?
Answerer: You ought to know, you dialed it!

Or…

Caller: Hello? Who is this? Who is this, I say?
Answerer: I haven't got time for riddles. You tell me who you are.

This next one exaggerates what an amazing person it must have been not to simply start barking questions over the phone when someone answers and instead clearly states who they were, and their intention in calling.

> *I once knew an eccentric man, who when he had got the desired number on the telephone did not demand fiercely "WHO IS THIS?" Instead, he would say 'This is John J. Poppendick, wishing to speak to Mr. Buckover.'*
>
> *His funeral was the largest ever held in the neighborhood where he had resided, at which strong men broke down and wept like children, being convinced that they would never again see the like of this man.*

Here's a discussion on which country handles phone greetings better:

Englishman: With all due reverence, my boy, I really think our English custom at the telephone is better than saying "Hello" as you do in the United States.
American: What do you say in England?
Englishman: We say, "Are you there?" Then, of course if you are not there, there is no use in going on with the conversation.

Here's a young woman a little clueless on technology:

A suburban housewife relates overhearing this conversation between her daughter and a friend next door:

Friend: How are you, Katie?
Katie: I'm well. I like my job. We got elastic lights and a 'hoosit.'
Friend: What's a 'hoosit,' Katie?
Katie: Oh, a bell rings. You put a thing to your ear and say "hello" and then someone says 'hello,' and you say 'hoosit?'

The word "Hoosit" being a play on "who is it?"

A quick note on the above joke. "Katie" in the book I got this from was "Katjie" a "Cape Cod" girl who used "yob" instead of "job." The "elastic lights…" sentence was "*We got cremated cellar, cemetery plumbing, elastic lights and a hoosit*." I can only assume these are either in-jokes I don't get, or the dialect and language of a not-too-bright girl. I left in "Elastic light" because I was certain it was a malapropism of "electric light" and just moved on to the punchline.

In the following joke, the doctor confuses his stethoscope with a telephone:

> *Wife, speaking to husband: My dear, we simply must get a new family doctor. He's so absent-minded that today he was examining me with his stethoscope, and while he was listening, he said "Hello? Who is speaking?"*

Here are two from a modern meme on the internet. Like the final jokes under "phone book" I include them because they are specifically from the older generation which lived through those early days and into the modern age. The first one refers to calling someone you'd like to talk to, but you had no idea which family member would answer the phone:

> *Kids these days will never know the fear of calling a girl you like at home only to have her father pick up the phone.*

On landline phones, to "hang up" you would literally hang the earpiece/handset on a button or lever that would disconnect the call.

Slamming down the handset on the phone to hang up on someone was so much more satisfying than simply tapping the "end call" button on a smartphone now.

Telephones: Wrong Numbers

As said before, there was no caller ID available— you had no idea who the number or person calling your ringing phone was going to be. That technology wasn't developed until the 1970s, and even when it was made available you had to pay for the service. Early phones also didn't have screens showing you what individual number(s) you had already dialed, so you could easily misdial a number and not know until the other side picked up.

The president of the phone company is awakened by a call.

"Are you an official of the phone company?"

"Yes, I am," the president responded.

"Well, how's it feel to be awakened at 2am by a wrong number?"

This next gentleman dialed correctly but fell victim to the fact that hotels and businesses often had a private phone network that would call the front desk if you didn't press a specific button first.

A guy checks into a hotel and he's really horny, so he figures he'll call one of the girls that advertise on the wall in phone booths. He pops into a phone booth near the hotel, finds an ad for one and when he gets back to his room, he calls.

A woman with a sexy voice answers and says, "Hello..."

He says, "Hi. I, uh, hear you give a great massage, so I'd like you to come to my room and give me one. No, wait ... I want to be straight with you. What I really want is sex. I want it hard and hot, and I want it now. Please bring toys, everything you've got in your bag of tricks. We'll go all night ... you can tie me up, anything you want. How's that sound?"

She replied, "That sounds fantastic. Now please dial 9 for an outside line."

He was speaking to a woman at the front desk, not the number he wanted.

This is a person dialing the wrong number and still assuming it was the number they originally intended to call:

A church pastor's phone rang and he answered it. Before he could say anything, he heard a voice ask, "Is this the Dickel Liquor Company?"

The pastor realized it was the voice of someone from his local church and responded, "No this is your pastor."

There was a moment's pause and then the voice said, "Well, what are you doing there, Pastor?"

And this isn't a phone call joke but plays off misdialed numbers for the punchline.

My uncle got two years in prison for a wrong number— it was on his income taxes.

Telephones: Long-Distance

Today you can speak with someone almost anywhere in the world, not just by voice but by video, for almost no extra cost at all. Until the internet, calling a place even a half-hour drive away from your home was long-distance and cost more money per minute than calling somewhere nearby.

This first one is just a silly question— the charge was for how far away the phone you were dialing to was, not your proximity to the phone you were using:

How far do you have to stand from the phone to make a long-distance call?

Here's one about a very tall building:

The building was so tall that when you called the top floor, it was long-distance.

Long distance was horizontal distance, not vertical.

The next joke involves charges for long-distance calling, and the fact that Pittsburgh had steel furnaces running all day long and was famously smoky and polluted during the early-to-mid 20th century.

A man from Pittsburgh, Pennsylvania was staying in New York City. He wanted to place a call to a town about thirty miles away from New York, so he asked the girl on the switchboard to get him long-distance and then asked the price.

"It will cost you 50 cents for three minutes," she said sweetly.

"Fifty cents! Ye gods!" cried the man. "I don't want to buy stock in the telephone company. I only want to talk for a minute or so. I mean... out in Pittsburgh we can call up all Hell for less than 50 cents!"

"I understand, sir," replied the girl, "but isn't Hell a local call from Pittsburgh?"

This next joke includes speaking to an operator to get long-distance, which you once had to do such as in the days of telephone exchange names. It uses the real placename of

Aberystwyth[1], Wales, but any difficult-to-spell place name will do.

Person: Operator? I'd like to place a long-distance call to Aberystwyth.
Operator: Could you spell that, please?
Person: If I could spell it, I'd just write a letter instead!

This one involves an operator telling the person there was a long-distance call coming in, and the second person misinterprets it.

First Person: Who was that on the phone?
Second Person: Some joker. They said, "It's a long-distance call from Japan," and I said, "It sure is!" and hung up.

There's also this urban legend:

A guy had an argument with his girlfriend right before he left on a long business trip, and he said when he returned, she had moved out of his apartment.

He returned expecting to find the place completely trashed but instead found she had moved out and the place had even been cleaned up neatly before she left. The only thing strange was the telephone had been

---

[1] "Ab-er-is-twith" is pretty close in pronunciation, if you want to tell this joke out loud.

> *left off the hook with some gibberish coming from the speaker.*
>
> *He hung it up and assumed he had gotten off easy... until his phone bill arrived with a charge for an $8,000, two-week-long long-distance call to the time and temperature in Tokyo, Japan.*

You could call a "time and temperature" number to get a message giving the information. This was helpful when setting clocks around your home. It was automated, so in this story the assumption is the phone kept the connection going for two weeks, the message repeating.

Telephones: Connections

As with any technology, sometimes telephones didn't work well.

> *I don't know why people are always knocking the phone company. I get a dial tone without any trouble— in the middle of calls!*

A "dial tone" is a tone that plays when the headset is picked up, letting the person know the phone is operational and ready to dial. Generally, you wouldn't get one when you got cut off in the middle of a call, though.

I'm not sure if any of this next joke was actually true, I wrote it the way it was written in the joke book.

The editor of the Japan Times says the telephone service in Japan is utterly bad. He said a lady in Karuizawa called up her house in Tokyo, left by the next train, got the call and talked to herself six hours after she arrived in Tokyo."

The book I got this from also misspelled Karuizawa, Japan as "Karuiwaza" unless it was trying to simply make up a Japanese-sounding place name. But then I have the internet today and they didn't.

The following refers to the busy signal that would play when the number you were trying to reach was already talking to someone.

First man, setting down the phone: I think I'll go fishing.
Second man: I didn't know you liked going fishing
First man: I don't ordinarily, but it's the only chance I have of finding myself at the end of a line that isn't busy.

Telephones: Payphones

Before car phones, cell phones and smartphones, if you needed to call someone when you were away from home you had to ask someone if you could use their landline telephone at their house or make a call from a payphone. Payphones were sometimes installed in a "phone booth."

Over the years the cost for a call in the United States ranged from 2 cents for a call in the 1920s to 25 cents or more by the 1990s. This joke is from the 1930s:

First Person: Has anyone got a nickel? I need to phone a friend.
Second Person: Here's a dime, you can call both of them!

It's a joke implying the first person only had two friends.

This one is about having to wait in line for a phone booth and is a "wives talk a lot" joke.

Man outside phone booth: "Excuse me, you've been on the phone for a half hour, and you haven't spoken a word."
Man inside phone booth: "I'm talking to my wife!" [1]

This joke depends on a Native American Indian Reservation where no one has a cellphone and there's a phone booth nearby. I guess you could have the chief possess the tribe's one cellphone, though— but because phones these days are assumed to have internet capability that would just beg the question on why he doesn't just check online.

---

[1] It occurs to me that this could be a follow up to the guy who was trying to call his wife in BLoomfield under Telephone Exchange Names.

The tribe's chief passed away before he could impart all his wisdom onto his replacement. The tribe then came to the new chief and asked if it would be a cold winter. Having no idea, he just told them that it would, and to gather extra firewood.

Late that night, he snuck out to the one payphone outside the reservation and called the Weather Service. "Is it going to be a cold winter?" he asked.

"Yes," said the Weather Service, "It's going to be a cold winter."

The next day he gathered the tribe and said with renewed confidence, "It will be a very cold winter! Gather all the firewood you can!"

That night, he felt doubt creep in, so again he snuck out to the one payphone outside the reservation and called the Weather Service. Again, he asked, "Is it going to be a cold winter?"

"Yes absolutely," said the Weather Service," It's going to be a very cold winter!"

"Well," the chief said, "if you don't mind me asking... how do you know it's going to be a cold winter?"

"We know because the Indians are gathering firewood like crazy!"

The punchline being that the Weather Service had been determining the severity of each winter by how much firewood the tribe was gathering, not by science.

Telephones: Car Phones

These days if you have a smartphone, you own a car phone by default. The jokes here refer to the phones actually built into cars, which were real from the 1940s until the late 1990s.

This quip discusses how maybe we shouldn't get surprising news while driving.

> *"I don't like the idea that people can call you in your cars. I think there's news you shouldn't get at sixty miles per hour: 'PREGNANT? WHOA!'"* [1]

It implies that the news would cause you to lose control of the car. Of course now we get all kinds of phone calls while in cars.

Generally, you'd get a car phone in addition to your landline. It would even have a separate phone number.

> *I had a car phone, but I sent it back. It was too much trouble running out to the garage to answer it.*

---

[1] Tom Parks

This is a funny image to have in your head but wasn't true. Car phones drew power from the engine, so when your car was off, the car phone was off and didn't ring.

And this is a suggestion that all cars should have phones so you can complain about their driving. The "1-800" number part referred to toll-free numbers that companies would use to allow you to order from them without having to pay a long-distance charge.

> *"I think all cars should have phones in them and their license plate should be the phone number. So you can call 'em up and tell them to get out of your way. Old people would have 1-800 numbers."* [1]

Telephones: Answering Machines

We still have voicemail today but it isn't as commonly used as a quick message can be passed along in a text. Before that when you only had a landline and couldn't be home to answer it, answering machines would record the message on a cassette tape so you could listen to them when you got home.

> *"The technological advance I wish I could get is an addition to my answering machine of a 'get-to-the-point' button."* [2]

---

[1] John Mendoza

[2] Alicia Brandt

And:

> *"Neither of my parents understands how an answering machine works.*
> *When my mother leaves me a message, she's actually trapped inside the machine. 'Carol? Carol?* Carol? *Are you there? Carol? I'm in the machine.'*
> *And my father leaves me these messages: 'Uh, tell her that her father called.'"* [1]

The funny thing about both of these jokes is people haven't changed. People still ramble in a message; people still feel uncomfortable leaving a message.

> *"If we're gonna have car phones I think we should have car answering machines. 'Tom's home right now, but as soon as he goes out, he'll get back to you.'"* [2]

The last part of this one reverses the common answering machine message, which said "[person] is out right now, and will call you when they get back" with "[person] is *in* right now and will call you when they go *out*."

---

[1] Caroline Rhea

[2] Tom Parks

Television: The Early Days of TV

Television was developed in the 1920s but really took off in the 1950s.

Boy: Grandpa, did they have TV when you were little?
Grandpa: Nope, the only things I saw on a screen back then were moths, flies, and mosquitoes.

He means bugs on a screen door. It's unlikely today to have a grandfather who grew up before television existed.

When television was new, it could bring in new customers to a bar to sit, drink, and watch the brand-new technology. This joke plays off that, in that the bars without a TV could still be entertaining:

A bar during the early days of TV put up a sign saying "We don't have a television yet, but come in anyway— we have a fight every night"

Early televisions had round screens because the TV screen tubes were round. They looked similar to glass frontloading washing machines. This woman confused the two.

An elderly couple was visiting an exhibition of appliances in the city and paused to gaze through the glass front of a demonstration washing machine at a bunch of laundry that was being swirled and splashed.

"Well," said the lady, "if that's television, I don't want it."

And of course we have this "dumb person" joke:

Q: Did you hear about the [dumb person] whose TV set broke?
A: They went into the other room and watched the radio.

Some young children believed there were "tiny people" in the TV. Cowboy shows were also very popular early on. That's the basis for this joke:

A TV repairman was trying to find what was wrong with the TV set.

When the six-year-old came home from school, he said, "I'll bet that if you clean all the dead cowboys from the bottom of the set, it will work again."

Television: Cathode-Ray Tubes

Early television sets were large and heavy because they used a cathode-ray tube (CRT), which would fire beams of electrons at a screen to create images.

Children were told to sit back a few feet from the TV, the reason given to them was because that way the TV beam didn't harm their eyes. In hindsight there have been no cases of any children's eyes being harmed during the age of CRT televisions, so children were probably told this more so their parents could see the TV themselves without a child's head being in the way.

"The tube" continues to be a common nickname for the TV, despite them being screens today and not tubes. The name of the website "YouTube" refers to that.

About the tube itself:

> *It's an eerie feeling turning 50. I never thought I'd burn out before my picture tube did.*

That's an age joke. Cathode ray tubes did burn out over time.

> *The television is one tube that it's hard to squeeze anything good out of.*

Comparing a television tube to tubes of glue/toothpaste, etc.

When you turned off the older, black and white "monochrome" TVs the image on the screen would immediately shrink to a dot in the center which would glow for a moment before fading.

> *People will watch anything if it's on television. You know that little white dot that appears when you turn it off? Last week it got an 18.5 Nielsen!*

The Nielsen ratings show how popular television shows are with viewers. Today data goes straight back to the company from your TV or smartphone showing what is being watched, but back then you were mailed a survey booklet which you used to keep track of everything you watched on TV for a week. At the end of the week, you mailed the book back in. Being a "Neilsen family" brought some perks like cash payments and gifts.

There are always jokes about the content of TV. Sometimes the programming was considered so lowbrow that the TV was called the "boob tube" - "boob" here using the meaning of a dumb person, not breast.

> *"I wish there was a knob on the TV so you could turn up the intelligence. They got one marked 'brightness,' but it doesn't work, does it?"* [1]

The various controls for the television screen were knobs on the set, with "brightness" meaning "giving out light." Now brightness is in the on-screen settings. It still doesn't raise the intelligence level of programming, though!

Television: Color TV

Color television was introduced in English-speaking countries in the 1950s and 1960s.

---

[1] Gallagher

I know a guy who pays no attention to the color of people's skin. Unfortunately, he's the guy who fixes my color TV.

That came out hot on the heels of the Civil Rights issues of the 1960s; the joke is a twist from "he's not a racist" to "he can't get the colors right on my TV screen."

Have you noticed most of the new TV shows only come in one color? "Medi-ochre."

This is a pun on "mediocre" meaning "middle-range-quality." And ochre; earth-tone colors.

Television: Cable TV

Early television was delivered wirelessly to an antenna, like radio, but could sometimes give a bad picture depending on how far away you were from the source of the signal, the weather, things blocking the signal, etc. Cable TV came through a cable to your house and offered many more channels and better pictures. Here's a play on the name, but about living in a rough neighborhood:

In my neighborhood, cable TV is a TV set that is tied to the radiator.

It's attached with a cable to the radiator so it can't be stolen.

Television: Watching TV

Much like radio, you didn't have a choice in the early days of TV— you had to watch the show when it was on, or you missed the show. Streaming or recording it so you could watch it later wasn't an option.

My grandmother would tell a story about a friend of hers who babysat for a family that had a television set in the 1950s. That friend watched a boxing match on the television that night after the kids went to bed. She didn't care about boxing at all, but it was all that was on and she had never been able to watch TV before!

This next joke says "Carson" for *The Tonight Show Starring Johnny Carson* (1962-1992), but it can be about any late show of the period, at around 11:30pm. It's about your TV watching habits, your chronological age, and when you have sex in the evening:

> *There are three ages of marriage:*
> *20 is when you watch Carson afterwards.*
> *40 is when you watch Carson during,*
> *60 is when you watch Carson instead.*

In short, having sex before the late show, during the late show, and watching the late show instead of having sex.

Television: Future

I don't really "get" this one. I came across this joke and was intrigued because it was a "future scene" in a joke book from the 1960s (before I was born) and talked about the year 2000 (which I remember clearly, from my late 20s)

> *Landlord (in the year 2000): And this is the bathroom.*
> *Modern Miss: Yes, now show me the television arrestor.*

My assumption about the joke is that Modern Miss is more interested in where to plug in the television than the fact that it has a bathroom, or maybe even wants to know if she can plug in the television in the bathroom (That's prophetic - we take our smartphones in there with us now, after all).

I looked up "television arrestor" to learn what it was and found nothing. I asked my retired electrical engineer stepfather about it, and he didn't know either. I contacted an online site with a museum of electrical arrestors (surge protectors) and the person I spoke to wondered if it was a typo. I'm thinking it's just a futuristic-sounding term.

Antennas

Antennas, also called "aerials," helped both television and radio pick up signals sent from large antennas. These still exist today in devices, but they are usually compact or integrated into the device. Early cordless phones and portable radios had a retractable antenna you had to pull out to get better reception. Television sets had V-shaped "rabbit ear" antennas or were connected to a large television antenna outside the house. Almost every single car had a visible "whip antenna" sticking out of it for the radio before they were integrated into cars during the 1990s.

> *A man was standing on a corner when a van passed by. As it passed, the connector on the antenna broke and the antenna hit and cut the man. He didn't think much of it at the time, but later he got an infection and died. The cause of death was "van aerial disease."*

It's a pun on "venereal disease".

Microfilm

Microfilm (also called microform or microfiche) was a pre-computer age way of storing lots of information and became popular starting in the 1920s until computers became the primary data storage system. By taking a photograph of documents and reducing the size, records took up far less space and could easily be copied and shipped to other locations. A magnifying glass, or a machine called a microfilm reader was used to access the information. This was a big leap because it saved wear and tear on original documents (especially old, fragile documents like newspapers) and saved space in research libraries, allowing the periodicals to go into storage.

Our accountant said he had a great way of reducing our bills. I said, "That's great—what's it called?"
He said, "Microfilm!"

Shrinking a physical bill to smaller size obviously doesn't affect the amount you have to pay.

This next joke is a pun off the name and is found in long joke lists poking fun at "new weights and measures" (Such as "52 cards = 1 decacards," "deca" being a prefix meaning "ten" and sounding like "deck of").

1 millionth of a fish = 1 microfiche

"Micro" meaning small and "fiche" sounds like "fish" with an "ee" sound replacing the "i."

Fax Machines

Facsimile or "fax" machines had their heyday in the 1970s and 1980s, sending an image over phone lines to make a copy at a printer on the other end, allowing full physical documents to be sent instantly to anywhere with phone access and a fax machine. They are still used today, but mostly in office and business situations. There are many jokes about fax machines, but they are often just puns on how "fax" and "facts" rhyme.

Here's two about being a little out of touch with tech. This first one is actually modern, it just refers to faxes:

I heard this morning that I didn't get the job as an IT consultant that I applied for. They said I wasn't up to date on technology. I was so angry that I went to the machine in my office and sent them an angry fax.

And…

Q: How can you tell when a [dumb person] sent you a fax?
A: There's a stamp on it.

The person assumed sending a fax was like sending a letter.

You fed papers into a fax machine, and I assume it was possible for your necktie to get caught in it by mistake, but teleporting to the destination is a stretch:

You have to be careful with a fax machine. Last week my tie got caught in one and a minute later I was in Chicago.

This joke is still told, but it dates from when cellphones were still new and faxes were still common.

Three men are out golfing.

The first man begins ringing and he starts talking into his hand. When he finishes his call, the others look at him funny, and he explains that he had his cellphone built into his hand, so he doesn't have to worry about losing his phone.

A little while later, the second man starts ringing and he starts talking into the air. When he finishes his call, the others look at him funny, and he explains that he had his cellphone built into his ear and tooth, so he doesn't even have to talk into anything.

After a bit, the third man pulls a roll of toilet paper out of his golf bag, pulls his pants down and squats. When the other two stare at him in shock he says, "Calm down, I'm expecting a fax."

The joke being the fax will come out of his ass onto the paper, and they thought he was going to take a shit. This is just as funny if you assume he actually was going to crap, just to spite the other two men.

Early Internet

To log onto the internet early on, via bulletin boards (1970s-80s) or by online services in the 1990s you had to use a telephone to call the server. The modem would play the sounds of the remote connection and digital handshake so you knew it was going well, but it was a very dissonant hissing and buzzing. That leads us to this joke:

Child: Grandpa? What was the internet like when you were a child?

Grandpa [making dialing phone noises]:
Beep- Beep- Beep- Beep- Beep-
Beep- Beep... zzzzz ...
[Making modem connection noises]
DRRRR DDRRRR ZZZZZZZD
RRRREEEEEZZZZRRRDDDZZZ...
Child: Grandpa, are you okay?

The sound was only played through your computer speakers during connection letting you know it was happening, then stopped playing the rest of the time you were connected.

Early on a descriptive term for the internet was “The Information Superhighway.” I even had a T-shirt in 1995 that said:

I got run over on the Information Superhighway!

America Online, many people’s first experience with the internet in the 1990s, notably would play a sound file saying “You’ve got mail!” whenever you got an email.

A [dumb person] kept going out to check their mailbox. A neighbor asked if they were expecting a special delivery, and they replied that their computer keeps saying that they have mail.

The person was expecting the mail in their physical mailbox.

I heard this in a routine on Comedy Central back in the late 1990s but have no idea what comedian did it. I'm putting it here, anyway. AOL Instant Messenger was a two-person chat system like texting on the early internet.

> *"Wouldn't it be weird if Instant Messenger had been invented before the telephone? You'd say 'Wow, you gotta try the telephone. It's like Instant Messaging, but you can hear the person!'"*

You could update the joke to now with "texting," instead of Instant Messenger, though.

Technology: Appliances and Devices

Outhouses

Sure as everyone has to eat, everyone has to use the toilet. Indoor flush toilets only became common in the early 20th century.

Before that everyone had to use a chamber pot inside their house which was then disposed of elsewhere or go outside to use the "outhouse".

This joke implies a wooden outhouse:

> *The farmer's wife said to him "I wish you'd fix the outhouse." He went and looked at it and couldn't find anything wrong, so he painted it.*
>
> *Later the wife said to him again "I wish you'd fix the outhouse." Again, he found nothing wrong, but he oiled the hinges on the door, just in case.*
>
> *A third time, his wife said, "I wish you'd fix the outhouse." This time, he took his wife out to the outhouse and asked what the problem was.*
>
> *She pointed down the hole. He looked in and said he couldn't see anything. "Stick your head through," she said. He did so, only saw the shit at the bottom, and said so.*
>
> *When he pulled his head back, his beard caught on some frayed wood. He pulled and*

yelped as some of his beard hair got ripped out as he got himself free.

"Hurts, don't it?" said the wife.

The wife's pubic hair was getting caught on the wood when she used the outhouse, that's what she wanted to have fixed.

The Sears Mail-Order Catalog

Before the internet and television age, the Sears Catalog was for many the first experience of being able to shop from home, even for people living miles from a city or department store. Their first catalog was published in 1887 and was the Amazon.com of the 20th century.

Toilet paper as an actual product started in the 1880s. Before that corn cobs and cloth scraps were commonly used to clean your bottom after using the outhouse/chamber pot, but also ripping off pages from old books, newspapers, and from copies of the free, several-hundred-page Sears Catalog.

People have claimed that the Sears catalog was published with a hole built into it to "hang it on a nail in the outhouse" and also that people complained when it switched to glossy paper in the 1930s "because it's harder to wipe with," but these are very likely "country bumpkin" jokes that while being passed around some people took for facts. There's no photographic record of the catalog with a hole in it for hanging in the outhouse[1], and I can't find any references to actual letters written to Sears regarding the glossy paper issue.

> *A farmer once wrote to Sears Roebuck & Company to ask for the price of toilet paper. He received an answer directing him to look on page 307 of their catalog.*
> *"If I had your catalog," he wrote back, "why would I ask you for the price of toilet paper?"*

Bellows

A bellows is a hand-held device you squeeze to produce a gust of wind, usually to supply a fire with air, before compressed air and electric fans made it easier. This is more of an adage than a joke, but there you go.

> *Q: How is absence like a bellows?*
> *A: Because it strengthens a strong fire and puts out a weak one.*

Just like in the old adage "absence makes the heart grow fonder" a bellows can fan a large flame or put out a weak one.

---

[1] It also would have been more expensive to print something with a hole in it. It is also possible that some people would drill their own holes in it for hanging in the outhouse, leading to the legend.

Carpet Beater

Until rug sweepers and vacuum cleaners became available, rugs and carpets would be taken outside and hung over a rope or a clothesline so they could be beaten, knocking the accumulated dust out of them onto the ground.

> *My Dad was an efficiency expert. He was so dedicated to his job that when I was bad, he'd lay me on the floor and put the carpet over me so he could beat me and the carpet at the same time.*

Wood-Burning Stove

There are still wood-burning stoves, but they're not as common as they once were.

> *Q: What are the three parts of a wood-burning stove?*
> *A: Lifter, legs, and poker*

This is a sex joke about "lift her legs and 'poke' her," but the "lifter" was how you lifted the lid on the stove without being burnt, the "legs" held the stove off the floor, and the "poker" was to move the wood around inside the fire without being burned.

> *A poor man did a great service to a wealthy man. The wealthy man said, "I'd*

like to repay you. Would you prefer a ton of coal or a bottle of whiskey?

The poor man said, "You should know I only burn wood."

The poor man wanted the whiskey; this was a polite way of not accepting the more valuable and practical gift of the coal.

Gas Stove

Gas stoves were developed in the early 1800s but didn't become popular until the 1880s, when systems were finally in place to deliver the gas fuel to homes in cities.

This joke, as I found it, was about a Southern mistress from Georgia who brought her "colored mammy" to Philadelphia and the punchline was in full eye dialect. Tell it as you will.

A mistress who moved to the big city found she could not be content without her old servant woman. She sent for the servant to join her, but the servant arrived right before the woman had to leave town for two weeks.

Before departing she only had time to explain to the servant the modern conveniences with which her apartment was furnished. The gas stove was the appliance which fascinated the servant the most. After the mistress of the household had lit the oven, the burners, and the broiler for her and felt certain the old servant understood its operation, the mistress hurried for her train.

After returning from the trip, she asked how things had gone with the gas oven.

"Oh, it's wonderful, Mistress," the servant responded, "Two weeks and that fire still hasn't gone out once!"

The punchline being that the servant left the gas stove running the whole time instead of turning it off when not in use, and the mistress is going to get an expensive gas bill.

Flatiron

Today irons intended for getting the wrinkles out of clothes are electrically heated, but before that you had to take a heavy metal iron and put it on a stove to heat it up first. This was also used to keep beds warm on very cold nights, much like a hot water bottle or a heating pad today, as implied but misunderstood in this joke.

When the thermometer dropped below zero the mistress of the house was much disturbed by the thought that the new kitchen maid slept in an unheated room.

"Maid," she said, remembering the good old custom of her girlhood, "it's going to be pretty cold tonight. I think you had better take a flatiron to bed with you."

"Yes, ma'am," the maid assented without enthusiasm.

The mistress, happy in the belief that her maid was comfortable, slept soundly. In the morning, she visited the kitchen.

"Well, how did you get along with the flatiron?"

The maid breathed a deep sigh of resignation. "Well, ma'am, I got it almost warm before morning."

She didn't heat up the flatiron on the stove before taking it to bed and instead tried to warm it with her own body heat.

Heating

In old apartment buildings heat was turned on all at once.

Our superintendent said he sends up the heat religiously.
And he does... once a week.

"Religiously" generally means dependably, but here they're making a joke about the sabbath day (The seventh day – "the day of rest"), implying he only turns the heat on once a week.

Steam radiators get bubbles in the system which would make noises called "knocking."

"There's no pleasing some people," said the janitor.

"What's the trouble?" his assistant asked

"A family upstairs telephoned me that they were trying to play "The Anvil Chorus' on the phonograph, and could I please regulate the knocking of the radiator so as to keep in time with the music."

The Anvil Chorus is from Giuseppe Verdi's *Il Trovatore,* depicting musically the gypsies striking their anvils at dawn.

Clocks and Timepieces

Before clocks and watches used battery power, you had to wind them up to keep the clockwork moving.

First Person: I left my watch on the stairs,
I'm worried it will run down.
Second Person: No it won't, it's a winding
staircase!

"Winding" being a pun on a curving stairway and winding up a watch.

In this one, the young man thought time was really flying when spending time with his date.

The young man was visiting his sweetie and was shocked at how quickly the evening was going. First, he heard the clock strike nine, then ten, then eleven. At the sound of midnight he said, "How fast are the hours when I spend them with you!"

"Don't be silly," she replied, "That's father setting the clock!"

This next one references sundials and winding watches. It is usually told as a Cowboy speaking to Native Americans.

A man is riding his horse along and sees another man lying on the ground, staring at his erection. He says, "Why are you lying there staring at your boner?"

"I'm telling time," the second man replied from the ground.

The man rides on and after a while he sees a man sitting on the ground masturbating. "Why are you doing that?" he asks.

"I'm winding my watch." was the reply.

Watches were fragile:

First Person: Did your watch stop when you dropped it?

Second Person: Yes. You didn't expect it to go right through the floor, did you?

They first person meant “did the watch stop keeping time,” the second jokes about “the location the watch stopped falling.”

Here’s one about looking at your audience while speaking in public.

> *When I give a lecture, I accept that people look at their watches, but what I do not tolerate is when they look at their watch and then raise it to their ear to check if it has stopped.*

This joke is that it’s understandable for a listener to check their watch to see the current time, but if they are checking to see if their watch is still working, they feel the speaker is so boring time itself seems to have stopped.

The next punchline is that the country they are landing in is behind the times (fill in any stereotype “backwards” country, I first saw this joke as “Saudi Arabia”), it’s the setup for the punchline which is outdated. Today smartphones automatically adjust to the current time zone, but wristwatches and travel alarm clocks had to be manually adjusted to match the local time zone, which was a hassle when travelling.

> *As we landed in [backwards country] the pilot announced, “Ladies and gentlemen, don’t forget to adjust your watches to local time.”*
> *I thought to myself, “How do I turn my watch back to the 7th century?”*

Back before we had smartphones connected to the internet, each keeping exact time, clocks and watches tended to be a little off from each other.

> *"My wristwatch is three hours fast, and I can't fix it— so I'm moving to New York"* [1]

The joke being it's easier to move to a new time zone that matches the time on your watch than to repair or reset it.

This next joke is about the time being off on a clock, and the silliness is in that on a painting, it really wouldn't matter.

> *[Dumb person]: I beg your pardon sir. I see you're painting a picture of the church. I thought I'd better tell you the clock on that church is ten minutes fast.*

Here's a joke that's a little prophetic about today's smart watches. It's notable that smart watches can do all these things— and more— these days, and with a tiny battery and your smartphone.

> *An inventor is struggling through the train station with two heavy suitcases. A man stops him and asks him the time. The inventor looks at his wristwatch and replies, "5:45pm."*

---

[1] Steven Wright

The man exclaims, "That's a cool watch!"

The inventor, happy for a break from lugging his heavy suitcases, stops and explains that it's a watch he invented and is still perfecting. It shows the time in multiple time zones, adjusts to daylight savings time, shows the temperature, current elevation above sea level, phases of the moon, and many other features.

The man simply must have the watch and offers the inventor $10,000 cash on the spot.

The inventor could use the money for more development and has blueprints at home to make another, so he agrees. He accepts the money and hands over the wristwatch.

As the man starts to walk away, putting on the watch, the inventor holds up the heavy suitcases saying "Hey, you forgot the batteries!"

Until the 1990s, batteries for mobile devices such as telephones were large and cumbersome. The joke is that the buyer didn't realize how much power such a watch consumes. It is left ambiguous if the suitcases are filled with batteries to regularly replace in the watch, or (my favorite) the two heavy suitcases *are* the batteries.

Fountain Pens

Early pens had to be dipped in ink for every few words written. Fountain pens have a reservoir of ink inside the handle, meaning you don't have to stop and dip the pen as often. Various fountain pens had been tried through history, but the modern, reliable versions were discovered and patented in the 1880s and 1890s.

> *"Purely by accident, I have made the greatest of discoveries," said the scientist.*
>
> *"May I ask what it was?"*
>
> *"I have found, "said the scientist, "that by keeping a bottle of ink handy you can use a fountain pen just like any other pen—without the trouble of filling it."*

The "scientist" is actually stepping backwards and using his fountain pen as an old-fashioned dip pen. It's like saying "It turns out you don't need a computer and email to send a letter! I can simply write it with a pencil and mail it using a mailbox!" Yeah, you can… but it's a little outdated.

Fountain pens and dip pens left little blobs of ink on the paper. An ink blotter would clean these up with a minimum of smearing and mess. The following uses "ink blotter" and uses several puns to reach the end.

> *Q: How is an ink blotter like a lazy dog?*
>
> *A: An ink blotter is an "ink-lined plane," an inclined plane is a "slope up," and a slow pup is a lazy dog.*

Fountain pens could be quite noisy as you dragged them across paper.

> *A husband and wife were in the dining room and from the kitchen came a dreadful scratching sound.*
> *"Dear,' said the husband, 'what is that scratching? It must be the dog trying to get in.'*
> *'No,' said the wife, 'That's no dog, that's the cook writing a love-letter to their sweetie."*

Moths and Mothballs

Older clothes were made from natural fiber like silk, wool, fur, and hair, which moths could lay eggs in, and then their larva would consume the garment leaving holes before turning into adult moths. This was largely a "winter clothes" issue, as you would pack those away and leave them unseen in the back of a closet during summer. You might not discover the holes in your clothes until it got cold again, long after the damage was done. Window screens started in the 1800s, but only kept birds and animals out, and weren't made with a fine enough mesh to keep most insects out until around 1900, so this was an issue well into the 20th century.

This is rare today as modern clothing is made from largely synthetic and bug-resistant fibers, and with air conditioning we don't have our windows open all the time.

Here's a joke about the problem. The wife falsely assumes moths would choose fancy clothes over everyday clothes.

Husband: You want to be careful about packing away your winter clothes, my dear. The moths are likely to get into them.
Wife: You needn't worry, dear. They are not going to bother with plush when they can get genuine seal-skin next door.

And this is about how the damage would often be discovered in the autumn.[1]

Autumn is when you have a religious wardrobe— holey-holey-holey.

It's a play on the Christian "holy-holy-holy."

Mothballs were a deterrent for moths until it was found that the insecticides in them were also dangerous, and modern technology solved the issue.

Autumn is when every person has a certain air about them — mothballs!

An "air" is a manner of holding or expressing yourself. Smells are in the air, and mothballs had an odor it would leave on the clothes from storage.

---

[1] A lot of these jokes would say "October," but in the southern hemisphere April would be the equivalent month.

This is about how uncomfortable it would be having them in your underwear.

My wife puts mothballs in everything, even my underwear. I put on a pair this morning and by the time I reached the living room I'd invented three new dance steps.

Mothballs are marble-sized, leading to the obvious testicle joke.

Q: Why do moths fly with their legs so far apart?
A: Have you seen the size of moth balls?

Spittoons

A spittoon, or "cuspidor," is a receptacle the users of chewing or dipping tobacco can spit into. They had a wide top which was easier to aim for and minimized splatter. It kept the floors of bars and saloons a *little* cleaner.

Spittoons were once more common for the same reason ashtrays were once common. Chewing tobacco makes people salivate more and swallowing the saliva could make your stomach upset.

In 1875, Georges Bizet's Opera *Carmen* premiered. At some time during the years following its release, people began singing this spittoon-themed parody of the chorus of the famous "Toreador Song" from Act II:

Toreador-ah,
Don't spit on the floor-ah,
Use the cuspidor-ah,
That's-a what it's for-ah!

And of course, actually hitting the spittoon when you spat into it was always preferred.

> *Two men show up at their favorite bar to find it's been completely refurbished and modernized.*
>
> *"I miss the old spittoon," said the first man.*
>
> *"You always did," replied the second man.*

I find this next one really gross, personally. It's the only joke I know that I'm a little physically repulsed by. But it's about spittoons, so… here it is:

> *There's a spittoon that everyone has been using throughout the night to spit their chewing tobacco into. One cowboy challenges the other one to swallow a mouthful from the spittoon for $100.*
>
> *The other cowboy agrees and tilts the spittoon to his lips. He takes a big gulp as everyone starts to yell in disgust. But the guy doesn't put it down. He keeps drinking the contents until the spittoon is nearly empty. Then he slams it down on the bar.*

The other cowboy pays him the money and says "you didn't have to swallow the whole thing, just one gulp."

The first cowboy said, "I tried, but it was all one big strand."

Saliva is stringy and sticks to itself… yeah, yuck. Let's move on.

Prefabricated Houses

In the first half of the 20th century, it was a bit of a fad to order a house which would be shipped to you in prebuilt sections you would assemble into a house yourself. Sears Modern Homes was the largest distributor, and actually hundreds of these homes are still standing today.

Here's a joke about a not-too-bright builder:

A man ordered a prefabricated house from a mail order manufacturer. He fussed and fumed and finally got it erected, but he wasn't at all satisfied with the results and wrote an angry letter to the company. The company sent a trouble-shooter to the scene, who took one look and told the customer, "You've built the house upside down!"

"I have?" he responded, "No wonder I keep falling off the porch."

Gas Meter

Today gas, electric and water meters have a digital connection that make monitoring usage and paying electronically easy. At one time, though, they sent a meter reader to your home periodically to check the meter's numbers to charge you for usage. In some places you used the meter like a vending machine, putting in coins or tokens to get a set amount of the utility. The meter reader would collect the money from the meter. That's the basis for this joke:

> *A father said, "Now son, start saving your pennies and put them in this yellow box. When you get five pennies, give them to me and I'll give you a nickel and you can put that in this blue box. Then, when you get five nickels I'll give you a quarter and you can put them in this red box over here.*
>
> *Seventeen years later the boy discovered that the red box was the gas meter.*

The boy had been paying the gas bill, not saving up for the future as he assumed.

Phonographs: Talking Machines

The phonograph, (or over the years called "talking machine," "gramophone," "Edison", "record player," and "turntable"), was invented by Thomas Alva Edison and greatly improved upon by others. Today most music is stored electronically, but phonographs used a needle that read small impressions on a disc or a cylinder and played it as sound.

The first recording that is preserved is Thomas Edison reciting the children's poem "Mary Had a Little Lamb." Here's a joke about this event, and how things often start working when you start getting frustrated with them:

> *Thomas Edison himself worked on the phonograph, reciting "Mary Had a Little Lamb" into it distinctly for nearly an hour without audible result. At last, he lost patience, and slammed the thing down, exclaiming: "Talk, damn you! Why in blazes don't you talk?"*
>
> *Then suddenly, the phonograph broke its long silence and squeaked out to Mr. Edison's horror: "Talk, damn you! Why in blazes don't you talk?"*

Early on, the idea of capturing a voice and playing it back was amazing and unheard of. The next joke mentions "ear tubes," which were a precursor to headphones— a pair of tubes you could put to your ears to listen privately. The song mentioned here is from 1892, and was performed by George Gaskin, a popular singer of the time.

> *A man from the country put the ear tubes to his ear, the machine started, and he listened to one verse of "Mollie and I and the Baby." He put down the tubes and said, "I'll wait until someone else comes in."*

> *When asked why, he replied he didn't want the singer to "bust his big throat just for him."*
>
> *Not believing the operators' explanation of how the machine worked he replied, "Look, just because I'm from out in the country, you can't fool me. You've got that guy down in the cellar."*

The man assumed it was a trick.

Early phonographs used a "horn" to amplify the sound, the large cones you see on old phonographs in pictures.

> *"What's the matter with this Phonograph?" asked the father.*
>
> *"Why, Papa," explained the helpful little son, "I heard you say last night that some of the records sounded hoarse, so I put a little cough syrup in the horn this morning."*

This one involves mistaking one new technology for another:

> *A farmer walked into the store while a song was being played on an Edison for the benefit of a customer. After listening for a few moments, the farmer said "Say, the telephone is a great thing, isn't it? That fellow on the other end has a great voice!"*

Eventually it was found that speakers using a membrane and electronic signals could better project the sound than a horn or a tube. Here's a joke ad for speakers that refers to going out to a musical concert— the way you used to have to experience music.

> *The advertisement for the speakers says it has "real concert hall sound." Every few minutes it coughs and rattles a program.*

Many early jokes about the phonograph were a play on the fact that it was a "machine that talked" and referred to the stereotype that women talked too much:

> *"I've had a couple of phonographs stolen," yelled a music dealer as he rushed into the police station.*
> *"Don't worry," replied a detective. "I'll catch the thief. It's a bachelor."*
> *"How do you know?"*
> *"Because no married man would steal a talking machine."*

This is a line from the 1933 Marx Brothers movie *Duck Soup:*

> *"Say! You haven't stopped talking since you got here! You must have been vaccinated with a phonograph needle."* [1]

---

[1] Rufus T. Firefly (Groucho Marx), speaking to Mrs. Teasdale (Margaret Dumont).

And comparing them to people who talk too much in general:

> *He's a perfect phonograph. He talks without thinking.*

This "generation gap" joke plays with how young women didn't know how to sew anymore:

> *Old Woman: How useless you girls are today. I don't believe you even know what needles are for.*
> *Young Woman: Of course we know what needles are for. They're to make the gramophone play.*

The old woman means sewing needles, not phonograph needles.

> *A guest evangelist at a church had been speaking over the normal time for a sermon at the church, so much so that his voice was becoming hoarse. Entranced by his message the woman turned to her bored son and whispered "Isn't he wonderful? What do you think of him?"*
> *"He needs a new needle," the son replied.*

A hoarse voice sounds scratchy, and the son is likening it to an old phonograph needle that needs to be replaced.

Phonographs: Effects on Musicians

Here are a few on the effect of the phonograph on live music:

> *An amateur flutist once stopped in at a fair where a talking machine company had an elaborate exhibit and showed such an interest in the talking machines that the attendant was certain a sale was imminent.*
>
> *"I see you have your flute with you," he said, finally. "Suppose you play a brief selection, and I will make a record of it, and you will then be able to hear the machine reproduce it exactly." The suggestion pleased the amateur musician, and the idea was carried out.*
>
> *"Is that an exact reproduction of my music?" the flutist asked when the recording ended.*
>
> *"It is," replied the attendant, "Do you wish to buy the talking machine?"*
>
> *"No," said the flutist sadly, "but I'll sell you the flute."*

The flutist feared the days of live music were at an end.

> *The Preacher: We tried a phonograph choir.*
> *The Sexton: How did it go?*

The Preacher: Nobody knew the difference
until the ushers went to the choir loft
to take the collection.

The sound was so good they forgot the choir loft was empty.

Phonographs: Skipping

Dust eventually accumulated on a record over time— attracted by the static electricity generated by the needle on the record. Records would sound scratchy because of this. There were no easy fixes— the record companies preferred that you bought another record. Another common problem was phonograph records "skipping" where a scratch or damage to the record would make the needle bounce. This either skipped ahead over parts of the record or skipped backwards to keep playing the same part over and over.

I bought a "Teach yourself Spanish while you sleep" record, but it started skipping after I had fallen asleep. Now I can only stutter in Spanish.

And...

A turntable fell on my head once, but I'm perfectly fine, perfectly fine, perfectly fine…

And...

As the plane took off an announcement came over the PA system. "Ladies and gentlemen, welcome to the first fully automated passenger flight. I am your robot pilot and once we reach cruising altitude robot stewardesses will be serving drinks. Please enjoy the flight, we assure you nothing can go wrong... go wrong... go wrong... go wrong...

This is a story a family friend who worked in radio had told my parents back in the 1980s. I am not sure if it is a true story, an urban legend, or a joke.

A radio DJ set up a few records to play in order while he went down to eat in the cafeteria, which had a speaker playing the radio station on the wall. While he was eating, a commercial for a radio reading of Herman Melville's "Moby Dick" started playing but the record began skipping at an inopportune time, going "Dick... Dick... Dick... Dick..."

Shocked, the DJ ran up the steps to the station, ran into the sound booth and hit the record player — accidentally making it go "Dick... Dick... Dick— THAR SHE BLOWS!"

Phonographs: Speeds and Sides

A record had to rotate at a certain speed to sound natural. Older phonographs didn't support the specific speed of later records and used a different needle than later, more modern phonographs. The "long-play microgroove record" mentioned in this next joke refers to what more modern record players call "33 1/3". "Long-play" is abbreviated to "LP," which is why people call records LPs.

> *My grandfather could not pass up a bargain. One time I visited him, and he was in a state of excitement. "Look what I got at a sale!" he said and showed me a long-playing jazz record. Grandpa wasn't a jazz buff— I don't think he even knew what jazz was. He pulled out his old windup phonograph player and put the record on it— I was horrified.*
>
> *"Grandpa, you can't play that record on your old phonograph! That's a modern long-play microgroove record. The needle will ruin it!"*
>
> *"Nonsense!" he replied. "It's a record, and a record player."*
>
> *We sat and listened to the cacophony of noise coming out of the horn of the old gramophone as the old needle tore through the new record.*

When the record ended, Grandfather turned off the gramophone and said, "Well... if that's jazz, I don't like it."

In the later days two common turntable revolutions per minute (rpm) speeds became standard: 33-1/3 rpm and 45 rpm.

My friend called me and said, "Meet me at the record shop in 45." I made it there in 33, which was "record speed."

Meaning "meet me there in 45 minutes," but he got there in 33 minutes. A little extra humor on the side— he was actually 20 seconds faster than 33-1/3 minutes!

Records had two sides, an A side and a B side. This joke forms a pun with "B" side and "bee."

The world's foremost authority on wasps is walking down the street when he sees a record in the window of a shop titled "Wasp noises from around the world." Intrigued, he goes into the shop and asks if he can listen to it. "Certainly," says the shop assistant and pops it onto a turntable.

The authority on wasps is confused as several tracks of insect noises play. "I don't recognize any of these wasps."

The assistant looks down at the label of the record and says... "Oh, I'm terribly sorry. I had it on the B side"

This alphabetical joke applies to both records and cassette tapes, leading to the CD (compact disc):

> *Records and cassette tapes had an A side and B side, so it made sense their successor was the CD.*

Dictaphone

A Dictaphone was an offshoot of the phonograph but specifically to record human speech for use in dictation. The person could recite their letter, etc. at any time of the day for an assistant to later write down. It's the name ripe for a penis joke that it was used for humor, though.

> *Secretary: May I use your Dictaphone?*
> *Executive: No, please use the handset like everyone else.*

May I use your "dick-to-phone."[1]

Typewriter

Typewriters are mechanical writing devices popular from the 1800s until being largely replaced by word processors in the 1970s and computers in the 1990s.

---

[1] In reading though so many joke books for this project, the old "businessman cheats on his wife with his secretary at work" cliché was very common. Having gone through so many of those, I found the upset expectation where the executive was turning down something sexual a refreshing change.

Pressing a key would move a mechanical arm to hit an ink-soaked ribbon which would imprint a letter on the paper behind it.

> *A husband and wife decide to use code to indicate when they want to have sex. They settle on the word "typewriter."*
>
> *One day the husband tells his young child "Go tell Mommy that Daddy needs to type a letter."*
>
> *The mother tells the child, "Tell Daddy I can't because there's a red ribbon in the typewriter."*
>
> *A few days later the mother tells the child to tell the father that she can type that letter now.*
>
> *The child returns and says, "Dad said never mind about the typewriter, he already wrote it by hand."*

The joke here being the mother was on her menstrual period, so the husband masturbated, this information passed through an unaware child. An alternative punchline could be "Dad said his secretary wrote it for him."

> *Q: Why are there so few [dumb person] pharmacists?*
>
> *A: They have a hard time getting the bottles into the typewriter.*

The paper would be loaded into a roller to move it. There was no space for anything larger than a sheet of paper, let alone a pill bottle. At a pharmacy labels were typed up and then applied to the bottle.

This is a joke about the things people did to waste time at work, all put in one place so the stereotypical secretary would type instead.

> *Salesman: This typewriter is equipped with*
> *all the summer attachments.*
> *Shopper: Summer attachments?*
> *Salesman: A small mirror, a miniature*
> *clock, and a thermometer;*
> *everything a girl must consult*
> *frequently.*

When I showed this joke to a friend they were confused by the thermometer in the joke. Think of how people obsess over the temperature at work: "it's too hot/cold." This was before a lot of offices had climate control, and going over to the office thermometer to check it regularly would waste time.

Videocassette Recorders

Videocassette Recorders (VCRs) really took off in the early 1980s, allowing you to record television and to buy movies and shows you could watch whenever you liked to.

The "head" of a VCR was the part of the machine that magnetically read or recorded to the magnetic tape.

Customer: Every time I put a tape in the
VCR the audio sounds scratchy.
Repairman: Maybe it has head lice.

Many versions have been made of the following joke

A [dumb person] decides to do something they've never done before - buy a dirty movie. They drive to the local video store and find a title that sounds exciting. They drive home and put the tape in the VCR, but there's nothing but static on the screen.

They call the store to complain and say, "I just bought an adult movie from you and there's nothing on the tape but static!"

The clerk apologized and asked, "Which title did you buy?"

The [dumb person] replied, "it's called 'Head Cleaner'"

A head cleaner was a video cassette which cleaned dust from the VCR head, with nothing playing on the screen. The person was thinking it was like "giving head."

People operated their main VCR functions just fine, but many people would not bother programming the clock built into them— the numbers would simply flash "12:00." Here's a joke about that:

Q: Why did David Bowie's VCR always flash "12:00"?

A: Because time may change him, but he can't change time.

David Bowie's 1971 song "Changes" has the line *"Time may change me / But I can't trace time."*

There were other features which were complicated to figure out, like having your VCR record a TV program at a specific time when you were out of the house. Here's a standup comedian thinking back on that as not being as hard as they thought:

> *"I got a computer. I wrote an apology note to the VCR for ever thinking it was difficult."* [1]

Computers

We're still in the computer age, obviously. Back around 1989, when I was about 15 or so, my grandmother said that I was lucky to grow up in the computer age. My response leapt out of my mouth in one of those moments you think of for years afterwards and are a little surprised at your wit and candor: "I'm not really in the computer age. I'm in the ugly halfway point where most of the adults are afraid of it and we have to figure it all out on our own."

I mean it was absolutely the computer age; I was a little wrong there, but it was the "zit-faced middle school" years of computers. As I write this, computers are everywhere and being used all the time— not even being thought of as "computers" in the traditional sense anymore.

---

[1] Elayne Boosler

Early computers were large, filled a room, and could only do simple math operations. It's a modern joke that:

> *Today the room-sized computer is small enough to hold in your hand while you poop.*

The above refers to how ridiculous that idea would be to people in the early days of computers "what has pooping got to do with computers?" and today we sit on the toilet with our smartphones. Related to that, people have been cracking this time travel joke since the 2010s:

> *Q: If you were to time-travel to the past, what would be the weirdest thing to say to them?*
> *A: I hold in my pocket a powerful computer with access to all the world's information, and I use it to look at cat pictures and get into arguments with people I've never met.*

Getting back to older computer jokes...

Big computers from the 1940s to the 1970s were called "mainframes" from the housing they were built in. Here's a computer size joke from the 1990s.

> *If you can pick it up, it's a personal computer.*
> *If you can't pick it up but you can knock it over, it's a minicomputer.*

But when you can't pick it up or knock it over, it's a mainframe [1]

Minicomputers were mid-size computers in the 1960s.

Here's one referring to the Garden of Eden story from The Bible.

Adam and Eve were the first computer users; Eve had an Apple and Adam had a Wang.

Apple is still a powerhouse of computers today. "Wang" is a euphemism for penis and refers to Wang Laboratories.[2]

Early mainframe computers had no on-board (built-in) memory and used "punch cards" to record data, which were cards with holes in them. Each card was one line of code, and the stack of cards had to be kept in order. These cards would be fed into the computer which would read them, and when the computer had to save code and data for the future it would punch holes in a new card.

I know a guy who was drafted and that same afternoon became a general. He was standing there in processing, naked, with an

[1] Mainframes are still used, but they're gone from room-sized down to the size of a refrigerator, meaning now you can probably knock them over.

[2] Wang Laboratories (named for cofounder An Wang), was an early creator of word processors and computers. They filed bankruptcy in 1992 and have since been absorbed by another company.

IBM punch card in his hand, then he drops it and a guy with golf shoes walked across it...

The joke above is that the golf shoe's cleats punched the correct holes in the card to give the person the rank of general when the card was fed into the computer.

This joke is about people having trouble switching from typewriters to computers.

Q: How do you know a [dumb person] *has been using your computer?*
A: There's White Out on your screen.

White Out is a brand name of correctional fluid still used today. It comes in a bottle with a brush so you can paint white over text on white paper that needs to be corrected so you can type or write over the change without having to retype or rewrite the entire document.

As mentioned previously under televisions, CRT televisions fired a beam at the opposite side of the television screen and children were warned not to sit too close because they might "go blind." Then came CRT computer monitors....

Kind of funny how we were told not to sit too close to the TV because we would "go blind," and now we sit with our faces right up to the computer screen and no one says anything.

Computer monitors used CRT screens until LCD screens took over in the early 2000s.[1]

[1] Some people have taken this a step further and pointed out that with modern VR headsets the screen is right up against your face. Funny as that step would be if it were true, the LCD screens used in VR headsets don't send out electron beams like a CRT monitor did and are safe.

Technology: Traveling

For most of human history you had two options for travel on land: Either walk, or ride on an animal. That changed with the railroad, then the automobile, and then the airplane. Most highway speeds are about 65 mph (105 kph) and human walking speed is about three mph (five kph). If you think of a place a 30-minute highway ride from your home, it would take you about eight hours to walk there if you ever chose to — and that's assuming a good pace and not counting breaks to sit and rest. This was how travel was for most of human history.

Horses

Horses and other animals have been the primary mode of transportation for at least 5000 years. They weren't a lot faster than humans on average, but you could run your horse hard and fast, provided you gave it time to rest and feed after. Even at normal speeds, they could carry a lot more weight and you didn't have to do the walking yourself.

> *A boy went running to his mother from the stable, yelling "I saw the man who builds horses! He was almost finished because he was nailing the back feet on!"*

The man was putting horseshoes on the horse, which give traction and protect the horse's hooves from breaking on hard surfaces like stone roads.

Here's a cheap horse owner:

> *The man was so stingy he put green-tinted glasses on his horse and fed it wood shavings, so the horse thought it was grass.*

This next joke is dated because you would use a car today.

> *Elopements are very common now. I read this morning about a young widow running away with a horse.*

To elope is to run away to get married without worrying about family permission. A widow is someone whose spouse had died. The joke here is the twist implied— the widow wasn't running off to marry the horse; the widow was running off because they had just murdered their spouse and they were escaping the scene of the crime.

The following is about how it still takes skill and experience to ride, just like driving a car.

> *The man from the city thought he could ride, so he mounted a pony. A moment later he picked himself up out of the dirt in a corner of the corral. "Man, oh man," he said, "she bucked something fierce!"*
>
> *"Bucked?" said the old cowboy, "She only coughed!"*

There are still jokes today about how women stereotypically take forever to get ready to go out, this story requires the horse though. It's attributed to 19th century humorist Edgar Wilson "Bill" Nye[1] (1850-1896):

> *Bill Nye, when a young man, made an engagement with a lady to take her driving [pilot a carriage with a horse]. The appointed day came, but at the livery stable all the horses were taken save one old, shaky, exceedingly gaunt beast. Mr. Nye hired it and drove to his friend's residence.*
>
> *The lady kept him waiting over an hour before she was ready and then, viewing the shabby horse, flatly refused to accompany Mr. Nye. "Why," she exclaimed, "that animal may die of old age any moment!"*
>
> *"Madam," Mr. Nye replied, "when I arrived here that horse was a prancing young colt."*

He was joking that he had been kept waiting so long that the horse aged.

Of course, used horse sales could be just like used car sales, good and bad:

> *A farmer sold an old horse but warned the buyer that she didn't look too good. The*

[1] This name in 2025 is more frequently associated with the science and television personality Bill Nye "The Science Guy".

buyer thought she looked fine and bought her anyway.

A few days later the buyer returned saying the horse was blind and kept bumping into things. The farmer said, "I told you she doesn't look too good!"

"Not looking good" for a horse that doesn't look promising and "not looking good" a horse with vision problems.

This one involves buying a horse on a payment plan:

Buyer: The horse you sold me last week is a fine animal, but I can't get him to hold his head up!

Seller: Oh, that's because of his pride. He'll hold it up as soon as he's been paid for.

Horses, being animals and not manufactured technology, each had their own personalities and quirks.

A man noticed a farmer's horse kept stopping, and asked, "Is your horse sick?"

"No, he's not sick." The farmer replied.

"Is he balky?"

"No, he's just a little hard of hearing and is afraid I'll say 'whoa' and he won't hear it, so he stops now and then to listen."

"Whoa" is generally the term to call an animal to stop.

A man calls a horse and a carriage for a ride to 110 State Street and finds the cabbie stutters very badly. When they arrived, the cab passed number 110 State Street and finally stopped at 120 State Street.

When the man asked the cabbie why, the reply was "I c-c-couldn't say 'wh-wh-whoa' quick enough."

The cabbie couldn't say "whoa" fast enough, so he overshot house number 110 to 120.

Then there's this:

"Would you mind walking the other way and not passing the horse?" said a London cabman with exaggerated politeness to the overweight person who had just paid a minimum fare.

"Why?" they inquired.

"If he sees the load he's been carrying for just a shilling, he'll have a fit!" [1]

He's shaming the person for their small fare by saying their horse did a lot of work for just a little pay.

Halfway up a steep hill, the stagecoach stopped. For the seventh time, the driver

---

[1] A shilling is a British coin equal to 1/20 of and English Pound and was phased out in 1971. Some countries still use the term for their own unrelated currency.

climbed down from his seat, then opened and slammed the rear door.

When the sole passenger's curiosity got the best of him, he asked why he was opening and closing the door.

"Shh! Be quiet! Don't let the horse hear you!" cautioned the driver. "every time she hears the door open and shut, she thinks someone has gotten out, and she starts moving more quickly."

The horse supposedly thinks the load is lighter, so they go faster.

This adage refers to the costs of owning and caring for a horse and compares it to losing money betting on horse races.

Money makes the horse go, but horses make the money go.

Some saddles have a "horn" right ahead of where the rider sits. Most first-timers on a horse think it's a handle to help you get up onto and stay on the horse, like a bicycle's handlebars— and it partly is for that - but it's more so for climbing onto the horse than for staying on. The main purpose, though, is if the rider roped an animal with a lasso, they could tie the end of the rope to the saddle horn to free up their hands for holding the reins to ride, instead of holding onto the rope all the way to wherever they were taking the roped animal.

At a ranch for her first horse ride, a woman was asked if she wanted an English saddle or a Western saddle. She asked what the difference was.

"A Western saddle has a horn, an English one doesn't," the rancher said.

"Oh, I'll take the one without a horn. I don't think we'll be running into much traffic."

This used the obvious pun of "saddle horn" vs "car horn."

A woman was driving in the American Southwest when her car broke down. Eventually a Native American Indian came riding along and offered to give her a ride into town. She got on the horse with him and the ride went fine, but every now and then he would whoop with excitement.

At a mechanic shop in the next town, she got down off the horse, and he let loose with a final "Whoop!" and rode off down the road. The mechanic asked her what she had done to make the Indian so excited. She replied, "I don't know, I just sat behind him with my arms around his waist, holding onto the saddle horn."

"Lady," the attendant said, "Indians don't use saddles."

She was holding onto his penis.

What's interesting in the setup of this next joke is the idea of renting out a horse and carriage to two men who don't know what they're doing.

> *Two city fellows went on a trip to the country and hired their own horse and buggy to go fishing. When they got to the river, they decided to unharness the horse and let it graze for a few hours while the two fished.*
>
> *When it was time to return, they had a problem. The two were clueless about re-harnessing the horse and the horse did not want to be re-harnessed, most particularly it did not want to have the bit returned to its mouth.*
>
> *Finally, one man sat down on the road and said, "There's only one thing we can do."*
>
> *"What's that?" his friend replied.*
>
> *"Wait for the foolish beast to yawn."*

That's a reasonable way to approach the problem—horses do yawn - the joke is only a little amusing in that they don't know the trick to getting a bit in a horse's mouth, so they have to play the waiting game. If you're curious, there's a spot to press on the side of a horse's mouth that usually gets them to open up.

Horses could be spooked, and the automobile didn't help.

The old lady from the country and her small son were driving their horse and carriage to town when a huge automobile bore down upon them. The horse was badly frightened and began to prance, whereupon the old lady leapt down and waved wildly at the driver, screaming at the top of her voice. The driver stopped the car and offered to help the horse get past.

"That's all right," said the boy, who remained composed in the carriage. "I can manage the horse. You just lead mother past!"

The joke being that a spooked horse is easier to manage than an angry woman.

Horses, being animals, relieved themselves whenever they wanted to.

An English officer riding through the park in full uniform, boots and horse equally polished, came upon a young girl sitting on a bench alongside the bridle path. He stopped in front of her and she exclaimed, "What a beautiful horse you have there!"

This compliment made the officer feel very superior and he did not answer but looked in the other direction as if something more interesting were going on.

"My, what a beautiful uniform you have on," said the young girl.

Still the officer did not turn his head. But just then the horse spread his hind legs and urinated, which splattered all over the girl.

"I can't say I think very much of your horse now, but you're still a fine man." she said.

He turned around slowly but keeping his head high, said, "I hope next time we meet under better 'horse pisses.'"

"Horse pisses" sounds like the word "auspices" which means "under favorable circumstances."

Finally, there is the old, tired joke that goes like this:

A horse walks into a bar. The bartender says, "Why the long face?"

The humor is that for a human to have a "long face" means they look sad, and horses really do have "long" faces, from their ears to their noses.

There are versions of this playing off the original. One has the horse and other barnyard animals starting a band [stretch to a long story] but something terrible happens [band breaks up] and the horse is left on his own so he walks into a bar, leading to the original joke, giving a story on why the horse might be sad.

Wagons

Animal-drawn vehicles – wagons and carriages, etc - date to prehistory. They are still used today but aren't very common in urban areas. Just like gas-powered vehicles, the wagons varied - there were many different wagons, and there were different animals used for power.

> *Q: What's the difference between a boy*
> *running after a girl and a boy*
> *running after a carriage?*
> *A: One chases the miss, and the other misses*
> *the chaise.*

To run after a girl is to "chase the miss," and the second part is about how you missed the carriage and the other is missing a common wagon called a "chaise," a pun for "chase."

This one says the person talks too much and uses horse and wagon terminology to express it.

> *Q: How are your cheeks like a span of*
> *horses?*
> *A: Because there is one on each side of a*
> *waggin' tongue.*

A "span of horses" is two horses, side by side. A wagon tongue is the large wooden beam that you hitch the horses pulling the wagon to. A "wagging tongue" refers to the speaker's tongue moving quickly.

Just like how some people judge others by the car they drive, people were judged by their wagon and horse. The "rig" here is a term for a wagon.

A new minister drove his two-horse rig up to the mountain ranch of one of his congregation members. At the gate he was met by a boy who stared at him and was deeply in thought.

"Are you our new preacher?" the boy asked.

"I am," the minister responded.

The boy squinted as he looked from the minister to the horses and said "That's weird. I heard Dad say you were a 'one-horse' preacher."

A "one-horse preacher" could be interpreted as an itinerant minister, preaching the gospel wherever he went for little money.

The tail board of a carriage is sort of like a tailgate of a modern pickup truck. It could be lowered to allow people to sit on the back of a carriage, resting their feet on it.

Mary was accustomed to having Tom stop by each day at lunchtime. She was feeling very horny, but today it was approaching one o'clock and no Tom.

One o'clock passed and still no Tom. Mary couldn't stand it any longer. She hitched up the horse and buggy and started hellbent down Main Street to find Tom. The tail board of the buggy dropped off, and a young man on the road yelled, "Hey lady, don't you want your tail board?"

Mary turned and yelled "You read my mind— get your ass over here!"

Tail board being a pun on "tail bored" which could be taken as a euphemism for sex. Mary is so horny she'll take the guy off the street.

For some time, a man had been expecting his wife to give birth to a baby, and one morning he telephoned the office to say that he wouldn't be there that day, as his wife's labor pains had begun.

The next day he appeared at work. "What is it? A boy or a girl?" asked his fellow-workers.

He thought for a moment and replied, "It was a bicycle."

The others put their heads together. Plainly the strain had done something to him. One of them approached him again. "What did your wife have?" he asked.

This time he cogitated longer but finally replied, "It was a motorcycle."

They went to the boss and told him about it. The boss called the man in. "What was it your wife had?" he asked kindly.

He thought hard, scratched his head, and answered, "An automobile."

"You're kind of stressed out with everything," said the boss. "Better go home and get some rest.

When he got home, he walked at once into the bedroom. "Say," he asked, as his wife looked up from the bed. "What was it you had?"

"A miscarriage," she replied.

"Gosh," he said, "I knew it was something with wheels."

A miscarriage is a failed pregnancy, and a carriage is a type of wagon.

Elevators

Early elevators were not automated and required a person to operate them until the 1970s, when automation became standard.

A drunk walked into an open elevator shaft and fell two floors. He was heard yelling, "What's the matter with these elevator operators? I distinctly said 'UP!'"

The drunk is assuming the elevator operator took him downstairs.

The following is a two-part pun joke.

I got a lift to the eleventh floor, and as I got out, the operator told me, "Have a good day, son."

"Don't call me son," I said. "You're not my dad."

He scratched his head, "No, but I brought you up, didn't I?"

On the return trip to the lobby the operator apologized.

I asked, "Because you're not really my dad?"

"No," they replied, "because I brought you down."

The following is some observational humor about the early days of elevators, having to tell the elevator operator your floor and even mentions smoking on an elevator – which is illegal now in most places.

Here are some things about Elevators I'd like to have cleared up:

- *Why do operators always send the car up just as I'm about to step in?*
- *Why must you face the front of the car instead of forming congenial groups in the rear?*
- *Why does my voice always break when I give my floor number?*
- *Whether big buildings hire operators that fit uniforms or hire uniforms that fit operators.*

- *Why does the big woman at the back always get off at the mezzanine floor?*
- *Whether you should leave the elevator quickly after your cigarette has burned through the large man's suit.*
- *Whether I could run one of those things.*

Ships

Early passenger ships were cramped and lacked much privacy, like being in a building you couldn't leave for a month or so.

> *Being on a ship is like being in jail, with the chance of being drowned.*

Before radio made speaking to other ships and the shore easy, semaphore was a system to spell out letters to other ships or the shore by moving flags in the air or blinking a signal light.

> *A sailor was taken ill with a bad attack of rheumatism while serving on a ship.*
>
> *The sick man was promptly ordered to a hospital at port, but after setting sail again the ship's doctor found out that the man was still on board.*

Angrily he asked why his order had not been obeyed.

"Well," replied the captain, "We tried to send him ashore, but a sergeant of police hailed us and said that on no account was he to be landed or we'd be fined £100, so we just kept him on board."

"But did you not tell them we had a sick man, as I said?"

"Yes, we did; but neither me nor the signalman knew how to spell 'rheumatism', so we called it smallpox."

Rheumatism is a pain in the joints. Smallpox is a highly contagious disease that needs to be quarantined.

Early passengers often got seasick as they acclimated to the ship. Today people take medications that help, and modern ships have stabilizers to minimize the pitching and rolling of the ship which was what would cause nausea. Many jokes refer to seasick passengers vomiting over the side of the ship.

A man was very seasick and was unable to have an appetite. His wife, knowing he had to eat something, met him at the ship's railing with a plate of food.

He replied, "Thank you, but just throw it over the side— it's going to end up there anyway."

And…

A passenger on my recent voyage remarked:
"'Tis better to have lunched and lost than
never to have lunched at all."

It's a play on "It's better to have loved and lost than to have never loved at all," from Alfred Lord Tennyson's 1850 poem "In Memoriam A.H.H."

Windows on ships can be any shape now but on early metal ships, they were all "portholes." They were round, and some could be opened.

The left side of a ship is called the *port* side, and the right side is the *starboard* side. You can remember which is which because "port" and "left" have the same number of letters.[1]

Q: Did you know that ships only have
portholes on the left side?
A: The right side has "starboard-holes."

There's actually no connection between "port side of a ship" and "portholes".[2]

Then there's:

---

[1] Bonus tip: "fork" and "left" follow the same rule when setting out silverware by a plate before a meal.

[2] A "port" is a term for a pass-through here being a window, the same way doors are sometimes called "portals," and you go through a sea-port or an air-port when you arrive at or depart from places.

First Person: My cabin on the ship was nice, but I didn't like the washing machine on the wall.
Second Person: Washing machine? That was the porthole.
First Person: No wonder I never got my clothes back.

They threw their clothes out of the porthole into the ocean.

"Steerage" on a ship was where the people with the cheapest tickets would stay. It was named that because it tended to be near the ship's rudder.

A woman was on her first ocean journey.

"What's down there?" she asked the captain.

"That's steerage, madam," he replied.

"Really!" she exclaimed in surprise. "And does it take all those people to make the boat go straight?"

Then there's:

A [dumb person], who had never been on a steamboat before, fell through a hatchway. Down in the hold, and being unhurt, they exclaimed, "Wow! The boat is hollow!"

Trains

Trains became a viable means of transportation in the early 1800s. They could move far more people and freight faster – and at one time - than any team of horses pulling a wagon could.

The first trains were steam locomotives. The car immediately behind the locomotive was the "tender," which carried fuel and water. The following two jokes play off that car's name with "tender" also meaning "soft." The first is a double-entendre about women's bottoms:

> *Steam locomotives are female because they have a "tender behind."*

And this one about a factory tour:

> *Picking her way daintily through the grime of the locomotive works, a woman visitor viewed the huge operations with visible awe. Finally, she turned to the young man from the office who was showing her around and pointed, asking "What is that big thing over there?"*
>
> *"That's a locomotive boiler," said the young man.*
>
> *She puckered her brows, asking "And what do they boil locomotives for?"*
>
> *"To make the locomotive tender." He replied without batting an eyelash.*

Just as how boiling meat makes it tender, so the young man was joking that the locomotive boiler (which boils water to create steam for the engine) made the locomotive "tender."

Because they were taking the place of horses, steam engines were called the "Iron Horse"

> *Q: Did you know iron horses only have one ear?*
> *A: The Engineer.*

A pun involving "engineer" and "engine ear."

> *The train had run into a snow drift, and the engine was butting its head in vain against a six-foot snowbank.*
>
> *"For once the iron horse appears to be beaten," remarked a person in a carriage.*
>
> *"You shouldn't call it an iron horse," a second person said.*
>
> *"Why not?" they asked in surprise.*
>
> *"Because it's block tin," the person replied.*

"Block tin" meant a block of pure tin, in contrast to "iron horse." Locomotives are not made from tin, but the snow made the locomotive "blocked in," which sounds like "block tin."

Obstructions on the tracks were common. This starts out sounding like a love poem but takes a dark turn. "Gay" here means "happy" - the homosexual definition started in the 1960s.

No word was spoken when they met,
By either - sad or gay,
And yet one badly smitten was,
'Twas mentioned the next day,
They met by chance this autumn eve,
With neither glance nor bow,
They often come together so,
The freight train and the cow.

This is a joke about commuter trains, which differ from passenger trains as they have many starts and stops because people get on and off frequently. Radio stations periodically tell you which station you are currently listening to, and the joke is how the train stops at a railway station and announces which train station it has arrived at.

First Person: We came in on a radio train.
Second Person: What's a radio train?
First Person: It stopped every five minutes for a station announcement.

A motorman is like an engineer, but instead of locomotives they operate streetcars and trams, which have carriages, or "cars." That's the basis for this joke:

First girl: Where were you last night?
Second girl: I was out riding with father in his car.

First girl: But I didn't know your father had
an automobile.
Second girl: He doesn't; he's a motorman.

Electric commuter trains started running in the late 1800s. Some ran using an electrified rail, some used an overhead wire. This woman is asking the conductor about the dangers.

Woman: Would it be dangerous, conductor,
if I was to put my foot on the rail?
Conductor: No, ma'am, not unless you put
your other foot on the overhead wire.

Doing so would complete the electrical circuit and would be dangerous. The image of her trying to do both at the same time is amusing.

Trains were much faster than long-distance walking or traveling by horse and wagon. It could still take several days to cross a large country such as the continental United States, so the train would offer sleeping accommodations on board. A "berth" is a term for any sleeping place on a transport.

The train was so crowded I had to sleep in an upper berth. It was so small I had to sleep with my feet sticking out the window. In the morning, I found two mail bags on hanging on them.

The joke is not so much about the sleeping accommodations — though they could indeed be small — but mail from about 1870 and up until air mail began in the 1930s was by train, and to keep from the train having to slow down and stop to pick up or drop off mail at every single station, it was placed in a bag on a hook which another hook on the train or at the station would catch as it passed. Then postal workers on the train in a specific mail car would sort the mail and prepare it in a bag to be dropped off by hook at appropriate stations.

This next one originally said, "car window," which had puzzled me into thinking of an automobile, but the intended meaning was a train car window.

> *"I think that fellow is really mean," said Marie, throwing down the paper.*
>
> *"What fellow?" her friend asked.*
>
> *"The man in the newspaper article has invented a train car window that will open and shut easily by touching a spring."*
>
> *"Well, I think that's great. What's the problem with that?"*
>
> *"Simply because now I can never have, when traveling, some fascinating man bending over me to open or shut the window for me."*

She's unhappy about not being able to be a little closer to an attractive man. I used "fascinating man," but the original joke used "fascinating drummer." I was pretty certain this didn't mean "plays the drums" and found out that "drummer" is a Victorian term for salesman— as in to "drum up sales."

> *There is a [dumb person] who says that they always like to travel by a trunk railroad line, because then they feel more confident about the safety of their luggage.*

A trunk line is the term for the main line of a railroad, and the term has to do with the trunk of a tree, and nothing to do with luggage trunks.

> *A passenger presented himself at a way station on the railroad, with two trunks and a saddle for which he requested checks. The baggage master promptly checked the trunks but demanded the extra charge of twenty-five cents for the saddle. To this the passenger disagreed, and losing his temper, demanded "Will you check my baggage, sir?"*
>
> *"Are you a horse?" quietly inquired the baggage master.*
>
> *"What do you mean, sir?" exclaimed the irritated traveler.*
>
> *"You claim to have this saddle checked as baggage?"*
>
> *"Yes, it is baggage," replied the passenger.*
>
> *"Well," said the baggage master, "by the company's regulations nothing but wearing*

apparel is admitted as baggage, and if the saddle is your wearing apparel, of course you must be a horse! Now, sir, just allow me to strap it on your back, and it shall go to the end of the road without any extra charge whatever."

The traveler paid his quarter.

A "cow catcher" is the V-shaped attachment on the front of the locomotive to move obstructions off the track without harming the engine. The following conversation is attributed to American humorist Artemus Ward.[1] After the American Civil War, the train rails in the south were in bad shape and the trains ran very slow.

"Does this railroad company allow passengers to give it advice, if they do so in a respectful manner?"

The conductor replied in gruff tones that he guessed so.

"Well," Artemus went on, "it occurred to me that it would be well to detach the cowcatcher from the front of the engine and hitch it to the rear of the train, for you see we are not liable to overtake a cow, but what's to prevent a cow from strolling into this car and biting a passenger?"

---

[1] Artemis Ward is the pen name of Charles Farrar Browne (1834-1867)

For the next joke, the Railway Regulation Act of 1844 in England required railroad companies to provide inexpensive and basic rail transport for less affluent passengers.

One such rate was "one penny per mile" traveled. The accent is important to the joke here.

> *First Person: Trains leave for Birmingham, 10:23 a.m., 6:23 p.m.*
> *Second Person: What's "p.m."?*
> *First Person: A "penny a mile," I guess.*
> *Second Person: Then, what's "a.m."?*
> *First Person: Why, that must be an "'alf-penny a mile."*

An "'alf penny" is a "half penny," which was a half of a penny. There were no half-penny per mile runs that I'm aware of, the joke being that they are assuming those two runs are the cheap trains, not morning and evening times.

Politicians would travel by train and speak to crowds directly from the train on what was called a "whistle-stop train tour." This let them reach many people and yet stay on one train.

> *Assistant: The train pulled out before you finished your speech, Senator.*
> *Senator: Yes, as I heard the shouts of the crowd fading in the distance, I wasn't sure if they were applauding me or the engineer.*

The senator here jokes that he wasn't sure if they were cheering for him in support or were happy that he was leaving.

Bicycles

First introduced in the 1800s, bicycling— like the automobile— was more of a hobby than a means of transportation. Today bicycles are the most widely used vehicles in the world.

> *Q: Why is the lady bicyclist of an amorous disposition?*
> *A: Because she is a sigh-cling creature.*

It's a pun on "sighing and clinging" and "cycling" and probably also a joke that women had to spread their legs and put the seat in their crotch, which they might enjoy.

> *Q: What article of the cyclist girl's attire do a couple of careless barbers recall to mind?*
> *A: A pair of nickers.*

The first part of the punchline is that a careless barber would nick the people who they are working on with their scissors or razors. Second, generally women didn't wear pants in the 1800s. Women who wore dresses could ride horses sidesaddle, but this didn't work on a bicycle where you need your feet on both sides to pedal. Women cycling would wear knickerbockers, which were short pants—often called simply "knickers."[1]

> *Cyclist: Take your dog out of my way! What right has he here?*
> *Owner: Well, he pays seven-and-sixpence a year for the privilege of walking, and you pay nothing!*

The dog owner is pointing out that he pays a fee to own his dog, while the cyclist does not for his bicycle.

This is a humorous "motto for bicycles" and could also be applied to the automobile:

> *Wheels rush in where horses fear to tread.*

This plays off of English writer Alexander Pope's 1711 work *An Essay on Criticism*, famous for the line "Fools rush in where angels fear tread," meaning fools will wander right into obvious danger. The above motto is saying things with wheels go where Horses are too smart to go.

Automobiles

Automobiles were introduced in the 1880s and eventually overtook the horse as the standard mode of personal transportation.

---

[1] Outside of the United States, "knickers" also means "underclothes".

The automobile has increased the mortality rate, created appalling traffic problems, contributed to juvenile delinquency, showed half of America to live beyond their income… but relieved us of the horsefly.

Horseflies are called that merely because they are larger than normal flies, however they do not depend on horses to live, so they exist no matter if there were automobiles or not. The female flies bite.

Horses were stolen just the same as cars, and this is similar to the above horsefly joke:

Professor: What is the principal contribution of the automobile age?
Student: Well, it has practically stopped horse stealing.

It hadn't stopped it, but it certainly slowed it down— in place of auto theft.

Driving a car was more of a hobby at first than a means of getting from place to place. This pokes fun at how motorists dressed when they drove— with a driving coat, goggles and gloves. Goggles because there were no windshields on early cars, and the gloves provided a better grip on the steering wheel.

Motorists are still expressing their indignation at a recent disgraceful incident when one of their number, because he could not pay a fine at once, was taken to prison, and forced to wear ugly prison garb in the place of his becoming goggles and motor coat.

This piece is a diary titled "My Steam Motorcar" and tells the story of the first (and last) week in the life of this person's motorcar:

Monday: I buy a beautiful steam motorcar. I am photographed with it.
Tuesday: I take it out, pull the wrong lever, and back into a shop window. A bad start.
Wednesday morning: I ran over a few things.
Wednesday afternoon: Took too sharp a turn. Narrowly escaped knocking down a policeman at the corner. Ran over both his feet.
Thursday morning: Got stuck in a ditch four miles from home.
Thursday evening: Arrive home. Back the car into the shed. Miss the door and knock the shed down.
Friday: Ran over my neighbor's dog.
Saturday: Silly car breaks down three miles from home. Hired a horse to tow it back.
Sunday: Filling up, the petrol tank caught fire. Wretched thing burnt. Thank goodness!

If you're wondering why he was putting gasoline (petrol) in a steam-powered car, that's the fuel which boiled the water for the steam engine.

"Horsepower" was originally a measure comparing the power of draft horses to the steam engine. Cars were also described with horsepower, something the average horse rider switching to cars could understand.

> *The only trouble with a 60-horsepower car is that every darn horse balks at the same time.*

The "balking horses" here is the engine, making the car stall. You could also view it as the reactions of horses to the car itself.

The rates being spoken of in this next quip implies tax rates, but motorists want the rates of speed increased.

> *People who are in favor of increasing the rates: Motorists.*

And of course, roads had to be changed to accommodate the automobile.

> *The narrow trails where two cars could barely move without colliding are being replaced by splendid wide roads where six cars at a time can collide easily.*

This bit is about a community that doesn't have a problem with its roads being unfit for automobiles, as it would deter cars from visiting:

> *"Many roads in the district are unfit for motorists," is the report of the Tadcaster, England surveyor to his council. We understand the inhabitants have resolved to leave well enough alone.*

This next one refers to people flipping their cars over and being pinned underneath:

> *An admirable improvement in motorcars is about to be introduced by one of our leading firms. Cars are frequently overturned, and the occupants buried underneath.*
>
> *In future, on the bottom of every car made by the firm in question there will be engraved the words, "Here lies..." followed by a blank space, which can be filled in by the purchaser.*

Meaning they would could be essentially buried on the spot.

> *Have a care how you speed!*
> *Take the motorist's case:*
> *On his tomb you can read,*
> *Requiescat in pace.*

That poetic warning plays with Latin. The "RIP" on tombstones, we are often told means "Rest in Peace," but it's originally from the Latin *Requiescat in pace,* which means "may they rest in peace." They are making a pun off the ablative singular[1] of the Latin *pax*, which is *pace*, and "pace" meaning "rate." So, it's kind of "Rest in speed" in this poem.

There were several different types of fuel early on for automobiles. Gasoline (petrol outside of the United States), alcohol, and kerosene. The motorist here is extolling his preference of those options, eliciting a response from the man he is speaking to:

> *Motorist: I swear by petrol, sir; always use*
> *it myself. Now what, may I ask, do*
> *you use?*
> *Other man: Oats!*

The other man prefers horses, which eat oats.

This is a complaint by drivers about their depiction in cartoons in humor magazines and newspapers.

> *A well-known motorist has been complaining of the campaign waged against motorcars by humorous artists, who never seem to tire of depicting accidents. "One common and ludicrous error in many drawings," he said, "is the placing of the driver on the wrong side of the car."*

---

[1] I'm not a linguist. Don't expect me to explain "ablative singular", but it's certainly fun to say!

But surely, in an accident, that is just where he would find himself.

Police officers didn't have cars with sirens and flashing lights at first; they only had their voices and whistles to tell cars to stop.

Police officer: Didn't you hear me call for you to stop?
Driver: I didn't know it was you. I thought it was someone I had run over.

And…

Police Officer: Why didn't you stop when I signaled you?
Driver: Well, it had taken me two hours to get this old car started, and it seemed a shame to stop merely to avoid a little thing like being arrested.

The original version of this used "flivver" for "car." It's a term for a cheap vehicle.

Then there's this:

An irate customer complained to her butcher about finding pieces of rubber in the sausage meat and demanded an explanation.

The butcher said, "It's only another example of how the automobile is replacing the horse."

Horse meat isn't commonly eaten— the joke here is the horsemeat was used as a filler by the butcher, and now they're using rubber as filler instead.

First Person: I see Smith is building a garage. When did he get a car?
Second Person: He hasn't got one yet, but he's got an option for ten gallons of gasoline.

I assume that the joke here is that he got a chance to buy some gas so he's preparing to buy a car. Gas could be hard to find in the early days because there wasn't yet a network of stations.

The following is how horses were still more reliable than cars.

First Person: I've stopped riding horseback and got a secondhand car.
Second Person: Because you need more exercise?

A joke about how a wife would always want to use the car if given the chance:

First Person: I thought you owned an automobile.

Second Person: I do, but I taught my wife to drive it, and now I'm back to the streetcars.

Speedometers (called velocimeters at the time) were invented in 1888, and the first cars were sold with them in 1901. This joke requires asking if a car has a speedometer, which would be an odd question today.

"Has this car got a speedometer?" the man asked the car salesman.

The salesman replied, "At thirty miles an hour the car exhibits a white flag, at forty miles an hour, a red flag and at fifty miles an hour a phonograph begins to play 'I want to be an angel, and with the angels stand.'" [1]

The joke being that the car instead of having a speed indicator it warns you for your life at each speed.

It took a while for today's railroad crossings which block traffic to come into common usage— until the 1950s. People would try to beat the train across the crossing "grade," so they didn't have to sit and wait, with obvious and deadly results.

A world's record is claimed by an unskilled Detroit man who recently took an

---

[1] "I Want to Be an Angel" is a church hymn published in 1867.

automobile apart in 30 seconds— at a railroad crossing.

The train destroyed the car.

Here's a poem about people who dodged trains:

There was a man who fancied that by
driving good and fast,
He'd get his car across the track before the
train came past;
He'd miss the engine by an inch and make
the trainhands sore.
There was a man who fancied this; there
isn't anymore.

I can't clear it up without ruining the poem, but "...make the trainhands sore" here refers to the train workers being angry.

Usually the jokes were about horrible accidents. This joke upsets that cliché making it about doing the right thing.

A motorist's life was miraculously saved the other day. He stopped his car at a railroad crossing and waited for an approaching train to pass.

Before electric starters, cars commonly had to be cranked to start them up. You would put a removable handle into a socket in the front grill of the car and crank it to get the engine started. In this, a father is telling his son about how future presidents did hard work themselves.

> *Father: Remember son, President Garfield*
> *drove mules on a town path, and*
> *Lincoln split rails.*
> *Son: I know Dad, but did any of these*
> *presidents ever crank a cold motor*
> *for an hour before he discovered he*
> *didn't have any gasoline in it?*

And here is a joke about replacement parts and car accidents:

> *"My brother bought a motorcar here last week," said an angry man to the car salesman, "and he said you claimed if anything broke, you would supply him with new parts."*
>
> *"Certainly, he said. What does your brother want?"*
>
> *"He wants a kneecap, some skin, and three teeth."*

Turn signals were not required on every car in the United States until the 1960s. Some cars weren't enclosed, so hand signaling to those behind you was easy. Enclosed cars before turn signals, however, you had to stick your arm out the window to indicate the turn. Yes, even if it was cold, snowing or raining. The hand signals were even once part of the tests to get your driver's license.

They make cars too low to the ground these days. Yesterday I stuck out my hand to make a left turn, and I'll never forget it. Neither will the policeman tying his shoes.

He stuck out his hand and "goosed" the police officer.

Service stations once had attendants come out and offer to look over your car and do some light maintenance (and hopefully charge you for it). Here are some sarcastic responses:

Attendant: Ten gallons sir?
Customer: Yes.
Attendant: Check your oil sir?
Customer: No, it's okay.
Attendant: Got enough water in your radiator?
Customer: Yes, it's filled up.
Attendant: Anything else sir?
Customer: Yes, could you please stick out your tongue so I can seal this letter?

And:

Attendant: Check your oil?
Customer: No, I'll take it with me.

Playing off of "checked bags" when travelling.

Just like today, it wasn't just the station attendants that were annoying, it went both ways:

Attendant 1: Here comes another I.W.W. customer.
Attendant 2: What's that?
Attendant 1: They just want Information, Wind and Water

The customer only wants the free services. The "wind" here being air for filling up the tires, and the water was for the radiator.

Here is a humorous musing on whether service stations were pulling a fast one on customers with road maps in pre-GPS days:

People are too trusting. They use road maps to get where they're going. The best way is usually the shortest way. The shortest way uses the least gas. Road maps are sold at filling stations. Filling stations make their money selling gas... what makes us think these maps are accurate?

This is a service station story that depends on a dashboard control that's been made obsolete with electronic fuel injection systems:

A woman drove into a service station to complain that her car was using too much gas. The attendant pointed to the choke, which protruded from the dashboard: "Do you know what this is for?" He asked.

"Oh, that," the woman replied airily. "I never use it. I keep it pulled out to hang my purse on."

Pulling out the choke on a motor restricts the air intake, making the motor burn more fuel to make up for less air intake.

Odometers started to be installed in cars around 1925, and track how many miles a car has traveled in its lifetime. They are electronic today but were previously numbers on rolling cylinders that dishonest used car dealers would roll backwards illegally to claim the car was newer (and thus more valuable), than it actually was.[1]

A [dumb person] was having a lot of problems selling their car because it had 250,000 miles on it. They brought this problem up with a coworker who explained "Well, there is a way to make the car easier to sell but it's not legal."

"That doesn't matter," they replied.

"OK," said the friend. "Here's the address of a friend of mine who owns a service garage. Tell him I sent you, and he will roll the odometer in your car back to 50,000 miles. Then it shouldn't be a problem selling your car."

The following weekend, the [dumb person] made the trip to the mechanic.

---

[1] Today's electronic odometers can still be "rolled back", but it's just more difficult and just as illegal.

About a month after that, the friend asked, "Did you sell your car?"

"No," they replied, "Why should I? It only has 50,000 miles on it."

The person was falling for the very trick they were trying to pull— assume a low milage car is more valuable and worth having.

I won't say how far the mileage has been turned back, but the odometer is in Roman numerals.

The Roman numerals system is thousands of years old, implying the odometer was turned back very far.

Detroit was once the automotive capital of the United States, leading to a fair number of jokes referring to its status:

You haven't lived until you've been to church in Detroit. Where else do they have bucket seat pews?

Most early cars used bench seats, which stretched across the car — like a church pew. Individual or "bucket" seats were introduced in the 1960s.

[Dumb person]: Tell me, is an "FOB Detroit" a reliable car?

In that joke, the speaker is assuming that an "FOB Detroit" is make or model of car, but it isn't. "FOB" means "Free on Board" which means that the delivery charge is to be paid by the purchaser on delivery, and "FOB Detroit" means that there's a delivery charge anywhere except Detroit. It's also the title of a 1938 novel by Wessel Smitter about the automotive industry.

> *You know how they charge $400 for a power seat so you can see over the wheel? Well, I get the same effect, and it cost me less— elevator shorts!*

Power seats are standard now. "Elevator shorts" is a play on elevator shoes, which make the wearer appear taller.

> *Don't you hate it when a company makes claims it doesn't deliver on? I bought a new gasoline that prevents stalling. I parked with my girl— it didn't work.*

Stalling— an engine stopping while driving— was a bigger issue in the early days of cars. Here, the speaker means that their girlfriend wanted to stop while "parking" which is a euphemism for making out in a parked car, and the girl probably didn't want to go further than simply kissing.

This next joke is observational humor, the joke being if you could open the door, you could turn their headlights off for them.

Why do people who forget to turn off their headlights remember to lock their doors?

Most modern cars have fixed this by automatically turning the headlights off and locking all the doors a certain time after the car has been turned off. It used to be that headlights would stay on if not turned off, which would drain the battery overnight. It was common to be in a public place and there be an announcement "The owner of a [description of car and license plate number] "...your lights are on" because someone had noticed it in the parking lot and reported it to the staff out of concern.

And on cars, it's worth mentioning an old standard of dark humor regarding a group of people who burned to death:

How many [group of people who burned to death] can you fit in a car?
Two in the front, three in the back and [number] in the ashtray.

This has been reused for multiple horrific events, the [number] for:

- Jews: *"6 million in the ashtray"*
    - The Holocaust, 1941-1945
- Astronauts: *"7 in the ashtray"*
    - Space Shuttle *Challenger* explosion, 1986

- Branch Davidians: *"86 in the ashtray"*
    - The Waco Siege, 1993

You can see how you could look up any fire in history and apply the joke.

The joke is now dated because smoking has diminished enough that ashtrays are now an optional feature in cars. Even current smokers tend to want to keep their car clean and ash-free for resale. The spaces ashtrays were once located are now occupied by power supply features for electronic devices.

Cabs

The word "cab" is a shortened form of the name for a two-wheeled, one-horse carriage called a cabriolet. "Taxi," and "taxicab" are shortened forms of "Taximeter Cab," where the taximeter was a device used to measure distance to calculate the charge for the fare. Taxicabs are still around, but the rise of ridesharing companies such as Uber and Lyft has changed how we hire a ride to take us somewhere.

Taximeters were originally used on horse drawn carriages called hansom cabs, the carriages named after the designer, Joseph Hansom. The passenger compartment was in front by the horses and the driver sat above and behind the passenger compartment at the rear of the carriage.

> *I never knew I was good looking until I went to the big city. The carriage drivers kept*

yelling "Hansom! Hansom!" whenever I passed!

A pun on "hansom" and "handsome."

> *"Now, Bobby," instructed the mother, "I hope you have fun at the party, but the weather looks rather threatening. Here's fifty cents for you, and if it rains use it to come back by hansom cab."*
>
> *A few hours later it was raining heavily. The mother was proud of her forethought, but when little Bobby returned, he was soaking wet.*
>
> *"Why, Bobby," she said, "didn't you come back by cab, as I told you?"*
>
> *"Oh yes, Ma!" answered Bobby. "It was great! I rode up on top, beside the driver!"*

The boy rode next to the driver in the rain, and not inside the carriage as his mother intended.

In the past, the only way to hail a cab was to lift your hand and yell or whistle for a passing taxi… or place a telephone call for one— leading to this old, tired joke:

> *Hotel guest: Call me a cab!*
> *Hotel clerk: Okay, you're a cab.*

Here's one which plays on hailing a cab by raising your hand and the fact that people once used hand signals to make signal turns in cars.

I put my hand out for a taxi driver. The cheap bastard could at least fix his signals.

A driver who knew their customer was unfamiliar with the area could drive a few blocks out of the way to pad the fare a little. Riders who knew the area would notice this immediately and mention it.

Here's a father telling his son that he is thinking like a cab driver.

Young son: Father, the world is round, right?
Father: Yes, it is, son.
Young son: Then if I wanted to go east, I could get there by going west, right?
Father: Yes, son. And you have a promising future as a taxicab driver.

Here is someone who found a way to deal with fare padding during a trip which stopped in London.

A man arrived at Euston Station London, at noon. He hailed a taxi and asked to be taken to Waterloo station because he had a train at 3pm. The driver sensed his passenger was from out of town, so he took a very long, winding route taking up almost all three hours. The man saw exactly what the driver was doing but sat back and enjoyed the ride among the sights of London.

The cab pulled up to Waterloo Station at 2:30pm, and the driver was all smiles. The man hopped out of the cab, darted up to a nearby police officer and asked him how much the fare usually was from Euston to Waterloo. When the officer told him, he gave the money to him and said "Could you please pay my cabbie? I've got a train to catch," and then walked into the train station.

Presumably, the cab driver will say to the police officer how much he charged and the police officer would be able to tell that the driver was padding his fare.

This joke shows a trick used by this cab driver to make some fares on a slow day.

"Say, Jim," said the friend of the taxicab-driver, standing by his cab, "there's a purse lying on the floor of your car."

The driver looked carefully around and then whispered: "Sometimes when business is bad, I put it there and leave the door open. It's empty, but you've no idea how many people will jump in for a short drive when they see it."

The people get in and take a short ride for the opportunity to see if there is any money or valuables in the purse.

The fare system is played with in the next joke:

> *I came in a taxi. The fare was $3.80 but the driver didn't have change for a five-dollar bill, so I had to ride around until the fare was $5.00.*

It's possible the rider simply wanted to get everything they were forced to pay for, rather than taking a hit, or tipping $1.20. It's also possible the driver was lying about not having change in hopes of getting a big tip.

Here's a farmer complaining about the cost of cabs.

> *A farmer returned from the city to tell his neighbors the wonders of the taxicab. "They call them 'taxidermy cabs,' because they skin you."*

Taxidermy is the art of skinning and stuffing dead animals into lifelike poses.

This next joke is about how the girlfriend doesn't want to walk anywhere when given the opportunity to get a ride.

> *First Person: How does he like his new girlfriend?*
>
> *Second Person: He says she's too expensive because every time she sees a cab*

she gets paralyzed from the waist down.

This joke plays off the fact that the "Free for luggage" isn't "free," it's simply included in the cab fare.

Man: Cabbie, how much is the fare to get
me to Latchford?
Cabbie: Two shillings, sir.
Man: And how much for my luggage?
Cabbie: Free, sir.
Man: Then take the luggage, I'll walk.

The man is being cheap by asking the cab to carry the luggage to his destination for free while he walks.

Airplanes

The Wright Brothers achieved heavier-than-air flight in 1903, and since then airplanes have become the safest and fastest mode of transportation, thanks to proven technology and regulation.

However, in the early days of flight, it was very dangerous.

Here's a limerick about trying to find test pilots:

A genius who once did aspire,
To invent an aerial flyer,
When asked "Does it go?"
Replied "I don't know,"
"I'm waiting for some damn fool to try her."

I found it interesting that the book I got this out of (and maybe the original poem) spelled "Damn fool" as "Damphule," as "Damn fool" was a strong expletive at the time.

Early planes stretched fabric on wooden wings because it was lightweight, but the fabric would absorb rainwater, making the plane heavier, in turn making it more challenging to fly. Here's a poem about that:

Little drops in water,
Little drops on land,
Make the aviator,
Join the heavenly band.

This plays with how long it would take to be an "experienced" aviator.

Man: Are you an experienced aviator?
Aviator: Well Sir, I have been at it for six weeks and I am still alive.

This quote plays on "raise" to lift something and "raise" to nurture a child.

"We can imagine Necessity, mother of invention, looking up at the sky all crisscrossed with flying machines and saying with a shake of her old head and a contented smile: 'Of all my family, the airplane has been the hardest to raise.'" [1]

---

[1] Harry N. Atwood (1883-1967)

This is a play on family history:

First Man: My ancestors came over on the Mayflower.
Second Man: That's nothing. My father descended from an airplane.

Early planes were propeller-powered before jet engines. This one can still be used today for helicopters and small planes:

The purpose of a propelleris to keep the pilot cool. If you don't believe me, wait till you see how much he sweats when it stops!

Early airplanes were open to the air, and it took a good ten years before they even began to install seatbelts.

An aviator taking people on short trips in the air for a small fee got tired of being asked the same questions. When two women climbed into the back, he said that on no account were they to speak to him, because he had to give his full attention to the aircraft. Up they went, and the aviator enjoyed himself, looping the loop and doing other stunts without interruption from the back.

Finally, he felt a touch on his arm and a voice said "I know I shouldn't speak, and I apologize for the interruption, but I can't help it. I thought perhaps you'd like to know Annie's fallen out."

Another version of this joke had a man going for the ride with his wife. At the end the pilot, without looking back, congratulates them for being so quiet and the man says "It was hard - I'm gonna tell you though, I almost screamed when my wife fell out."

Here's one on jet aircraft testing:

Two buzzards were flying over the desert when a jet-propelled plane sped by them, its exhaust spouting flame and smoke. As it went out of sight, one of the buzzards turned to the other and remarked, "That bird was really in a hurry."

The other replied, "You'd be in a hurry too, if your ass was on fire."

I have seen this previous one cleaned up with "tail on fire," too.

By the 1950s, air travel surpassed passenger train travel and trains never recovered. This led to airplanes being the butt of some railroad jokes.

This plays on how when airports are busy, planes would have to fly in circles waiting for permission to land on a limited number of runways.

People complain about railroads, but I've never spent three hours on one circling the station.

And this is about how trains are "safer."

As a railroad engineer, I've been through six train crashes; yet I've never met a pilot who has been through six plane crashes.

Crashing airplanes are generally harder to survive that a train crash, what with dropping from a great height and all.

These days planes have a large fuel capacity and can make it well over a thousand miles without refueling. In the early days range was limited, and they had to land often to refuel.

Two men were flying across the United States. At each stop, a little cart was brought out to refuel the plane. After a few stops, the first man looked at his watch and said "Hey, we're making good time."

The second man said, "Yeah— and that cart is, too!"

The man thought it was the same cart at every airport, somehow getting to each stop ahead of them.

In the early days of flight travel, attractive young white single women[1] were hired as stewardesses.[2] The

---

[1] The first black flight attendant in the United States was Ruth Carol Taylor, who was let go six months later because of Mohawk Airline's marriage ban, which was once common in the industry.

[2] My wife is a flight attendant and points out that now they are hired more according to physical capability and personality more than

following takes a "busy airport" joke and then turns it into a "stewardesses are sexy" joke.

> *There's one problem with air travel. Over every airport in the US, things are stacked. They are called stewardesses.*

Flying is common enough nowadays that most everyone is aware that your ears pop when the pressure changes in the plane. Chewing works the muscles around your ears and can equalize the air pressure if your ears have trouble popping. Ear plugs also work to maintain the pressure in your ear.

This passenger had the right idea with the gum, but the wrong usage.

> *As an airliner was flying over the Rocky Mountains, the stewardess distributed chewing gum to the passengers, explaining that it would keep their ears from popping at high altitude.*
>
> *When the plane landed, one of the passengers rushed to the stewardess and said "My wife is picking me up soon. How do I get the gum out of my ears?"*

---

appearance. They are no longer called "stewardesses" today, men are included now, and there is more to the job than serving drinks and snacks. Among other things it includes training to respond to threats on the plane and for medical emergencies in flight.

Taking advantage of people's fear of flying, beginning in the 1950s there were insurance kiosks at airports which made money off nervous fliers. This faded on its own as it became clearer that flying was safe.

> *You have to worry at the airport when you see that the insurance machine is sold out!*

And…

> *I'm giving up on flying. I was at the airport and saw a sign: "Take out insurance." I thought if the lobby is that dangerous, imagine what it's like on the plane.* [1]

Long flights would offer an in-flight movie, but cheaper flights wouldn't. The following joke was about how drive-in theaters had large screens you might be able to see from the airplane.

> *I took an economy flight. There wasn't an in-flight movie, but they flew low over drive-ins.* [2]

This next one refers to the fact that before turn signals were put on cars, you had to put your arm out the window to signal a turn.

---

[1] Corbett Monica

[2] Red Buttons

My last flight was a beauty. The pilot made a left turn; he put his arm out the window. [1]

The following two are plays on airlines and slogans. United Airlines first used "Fly the friendly skies" in 1965, leading to this joke, which switches two words to make it about asking passengers to keep their pants on, "fly" being a term for zipper:

Did you hear about the beautiful United Airlines stewardess who had to ask the passengers to "'sky' their friendly flies?"

This mixes two airline names and makes it into a joke about telling jokes. Alitalia was the largest airline in Italy (pronounced "All-ee-tall-yah") and "El Al" is the airline for Israel. It mashes the two names together.

Did you hear that Alitalia and El Al were merging to form a new airline? It's going to be called "Well, I'll-a-tell-ya."

Old observational comedy skits would set up a joke by saying "you know what's strange about [thing]?" then saying "Well, I'll tell ya," to signal the beginning of the joke. Modern observational humor doesn't use this signal for the audience much anymore.

The Concorde was a supersonic passenger jet aircraft from 1976 to 2003. Normal airplanes go from New York to

---

[1] Rodney Dangerfield

London in seven hours, the Concorde could do that in three and a half hours, half the time of a standard plane.

> *The Concorde is great. It travels at twice the speed of sound. Which is fun except you can't hear the in-flight movie until two hours after you land.* [1]

This joke plays with the true speed of the plane "twice the speed of sound" as if you could go faster than the sound of the movie you are watching, which is untrue. The sound would be right there in the same air you are breathing. [2]

The following became very dated after the events of the September 11th attacks. Airlines once used real silverware for inflight meals before they switched to disposable plasticware. The speaker here is talking about being randomly patted down while passing through security.

> *Ever been frisked on a plane trip? They frisk you, and then on the plane they give everybody a steak knife!* [3]

Before 9/11, when the terrorists took over the plane using bladed box cutters, the concern was more about a gun or a bomb than a knife. Some airlines have returned to using silverware but under very strict rules.

---

[1] Howie Mandel

[2] If you're curious, the Concorde didn't actually show in-flight movies. It served its passengers luxury food and drink, but the plane itself was actually cramped and noisy.

[3] Shelly Berman

Events: 1850-1900

Irish Famine (1845-1852)

From 1845-1852, a blight affected potato crops in Ireland, ruining them and leading to widespread starvation in Ireland which affected the rest of Europe, also.

> *Q: How many potatoes does it take to kill an Irishman?*
> A: Zero.

In terms of humor history, the masses of Irish leaving Ireland due to the famine for other places caused the wave of "Irishmen as the butt of jokes" in the 1800s.

California Gold Rush (1848–1855)

This is cute, in that by the end you learn the "12-pound nugget" the coal miner was bragging about was actually his newborn, and the responses from the sister are filled with fun double-entendres regarding sex and mining.

> *In a gold-mining district, a claim-worker, Mr. Brown, received news with which he was so delighted he ran down the street telling everybody he met that he had found "a twelve-pound gold nugget as good as any to be found in America."*
>
> *Such news was without a precedent even in that locality, where men were striking it*

rich every day, so the local newspaper sent a reporter to get the particulars. Mrs. Brown's elder sister, a witty woman, fond of jokes, happened to answer the bell. This is the conversation that followed:

Reporter: Does Mr. Brown live here?
Sister: Yes.
Reporter: May I speak with him?
Sister: I'm sorry, but he's not in just now. Is there anything I can do?
Reporter: Well, I understand he found a twelve-pound nugget.
Sister: [Seeing the situation] Why, yes.
Reporter: Can you show me the exact spot where he found it?
Sister: I'm afraid Mr. Brown would never consent to that, as it is private.
Reporter: Is the hole very far from here?
Sister: No, it is quite handy.
Reporter: Has Mr. Brown been working the claim very long?
Sister: Only about ten months.
Reporter: Was he the first to work it?
Sister: Well, he's told me he believed he was.
Reporter: Was the work difficult?
Sister: It was at first, but it was easier after a while.
Reporter: Has he got to the bottom yet?
Sister: Not yet, I believe, but very near.

Reporter: Do you think there are any more nuggets?

Sister: Doubtless, if the claim is properly worked.

Reporter: Has he worked it since he found the nugget?

Sister: No. But last night I heard Mrs. Brown tell him it was time to start again.

Reporter: I suppose he works secretly.

Sister: Yes, mostly at night.

Reporter: Did he have any help?

Sister: Well, Mrs. Brown did her level best, I am sure.

Reporter: Do you think he would consider parting with the claim?

Sister: No. He finds too much pleasure working it himself.

Reporter: Did he blast with nitroglycerine or did he do it all by hand?

Sister: I believe he did some of it by hand. He just kept on digging, though I believe he used Vaseline.

Reporter: Has he widened the hole any?

Sister: Yes, a little.

Reporter: Is he going to improve the mine?

Sister: Well, he said he would whitewash it.

Reporter: Does he always work alone at night?

Sister: No. Mrs. Brown holds the tool for him and they go fifty-fifty.

Reporter: Would you mind showing me the nugget?
Sister: Not at all!
...And she brought a baby to the door.

The American Civil War (1861-1865)

People still debate and discuss if the American Civil War[1] was fought over slavery or state's rights.

This joke refers the war being about slavery, and the colored man is pointing out why he's not picking a side.

A white soldier asked a colored man why he didn't enlist to fight.

"Well," the man said, "did you ever see two dogs fighting over a bone?"

"Certainly," the white soldier replied.

"Well, have you ever seen the bone fight?"

"No," answered the white soldier.

"Well, I'm the bone."

This next joke occurs after the war, when tours had begun of famous battlefields. The tour guide is assuming his group is from the North.

Guide: Yes sir, it was right here the Rebels began to run—

---

[1] Also called "The War Between the States," as a friend of mine from Arkansas keeps reminding me.

Tourist [interrupting him]: Come, now!
Run? I was a Rebel myself and I
don't believe they ran.
Guide: Hold on, let me finish. I didn't say
which way they ran— they ran
towards the enemy!

This sexual poem references the American Civil War in its title, and the ending refers to Northern Union Soldier's uniforms (blue) and the Southern Confederacy's uniforms (gray).

<u>The Civil Whore</u>
The Postman came
On the first of May,
The Policeman came
The very next day,
Nine months later,
There was hell to pay—
Who fired the shot?
The Blue or the Gray?

Here questioning if the man who "fired the shot" (got the girl pregnant) was the police officer – "the blue" - or the postman — US postal workers started wearing uniforms in 1868, and they wore gray uniforms – "the gray".

The Johnstown Flood (1889)

On May 31, 1889, the South Fork Dam broke under heavy rain and flooded the town of Johnstown, Pennsylvania, killing over 2,000 people.

Fourteen years later, on December 30, 1903, there was a fire at the Iroquois Theater in Chicago, killing over 600 people. The fire was caused by an arc light, and most deaths were caused by faulty emergency exits. Afterwards theaters faced smaller crowds and ticket revenue so out of safety they warned people not to smoke in the theater for safety reasons.[1] Smoking was so common you could do it almost everywhere back then and people didn't like the inconvenience of sitting through a theater production without being able to smoke, even if they understood why.

A common warning before a show was "Don't smoke! Remember the Iroquois Theater!" This led to a parody saying, which became so popular in the early 1900s that many didn't remember where it came from or why it was even said:

> *Don't spit on the floor! Remember the Johnstown Flood!*

It's a playful reference to the admonitions to not smoke in theaters. It's like people cracking jokes about safety

---

[1] I also assume that simply telling people not to smoke was much cheaper than fixing their exits. To be fair, they also were fighting a battle with people sneaking in through the exits to watch for free, so this wasn't *entirely* "theater owners don't care about the safety of their customers." They *were* playing the odds, which were usually in their favor… but unfortunately not always.

instruction demonstrations on an airplane before takeoff — every passenger understands why they have to sit through it before the flight, but the fact that it gets repetitive makes it easy fuel for humor.

Events: 1900-1925

Carrie Nation (1900)

Carrie Nation was a famous Temperance reformer who felt she received a calling from God in 1900 to warn people about the perils of alcohol. She was arrested over thirty times for trashing bars using an axe, prompting this popular bar signage:

All nations are welcome except Carrie!

Hopalong Cassidy (1904)

Hopalong Cassidy is a fictional cowboy from a series of short stories and novels by Clarence E. Mulford, starting in 1904. The character was called "Hopalong" because he had been shot in the leg and walked with a limp. The character's popularity peaked in the 1950s.

Q: What do you get if you cross a cowboy with a stew?
A: Hopalong Casserole

It's a bit of a stretch, but the biggest shock for me was that this appeared in a children's joke book published in 2000, fifty years after Hopalong's heyday. I truly doubt many kids got the reference, but I can hope it encouraged them to look back at old westerns.

The Thaw/White shooting (1906)

On June 25, 1906, Henry Thaw, a millionaire heir, fatally shot the architect Stanford White in a crowded rooftop theater. Thaw had a history of mental issues and was obsessed with his own wife, Evelyn. Stanford White had been known to drug and then rape women and had done so years previously with Evelyn.

The shooting and trial filled newspapers for years as both White and Thaw had scandalous backgrounds. The trial was widely publicized as "the trial of the century." [1]

> *Q: When did Evelyn Nesbit Thaw really love her husband?*
> *A: When he shot White.*

It's a sex joke. When he "shot white," he ejaculated, playing off "shooting White." It could also be interpreted that she really knew he loved her when he killed White, which was doubtless Thaw's intention.

Let Me Call You Sweetheart (1910)

"Let me call you Sweetheart" was a popular song by Leo Friedman and Beth Slater Whitson, published in 1910.

---

[1] In case you are wondering what constitutes a "trial of the century" it's just a saying in the media to sensationalize a story. There were at least thirty court cases in the 20th century which were described in the media as "the trial of the century" to attract readers. The first time I saw the term in a news article in the early 2000's I remember chuckling to myself about how presumptive it was to assume we were having our "trial of the century" so early in the century.

Q: Did you know they wrote a song about
what our customers say when we call
for payment?
A: "Let me stall you sweetheart."

The Titanic (1912)

On April 15, 1912, the passenger ship Titanic hit an iceberg on its maiden voyage and sank, killing over 1,500 passengers and crew.

Q: What do you get when you cross the
Atlantic with the Titanic?
A: Halfway.

The Titanic crossed the Atlantic and sank midway through its voyage.

85 years later, in 1997, a major Hollywood movie about the disaster titled *Titanic* was released to great acclaim, leading to the joke:

My grandfather tried to warn everyone that the Titanic was going to sink. He kept yelling right up until security escorted him out of the theater.

Two years later, a horror film was released about a boy who could see ghosts.

Q: What do the films Titanic (1997) and The Sixth Sense (1999) have in common?
A: "Icy dead people"

A gripping scene in *Titanic* was of the frozen corpses floating in the water after the sinking, and a famous line from *The Sixth Sense* was "I see dead people," of which "icy dead people" is a pun.

It's a Long Way to Tipperary (1912)

"It's a Long Way to Tipperary" is a music hall song released in 1912. It describes an Irishman who wishes to return to his love, back in the town of Tipperary, Ireland. In 1914 it became a common marching song in World War I.

My cab driver thought I was going to Tipperary. He kept taking the long way.

The driver above was taking "the long way" to pad his fare.

I'm telling this next joke the way I originally heard it, but I know that a lot of people tell the same joke only about a bird trying to fly.

A woman answers her door to find a door-to-door salesman. She says she doesn't want to buy anything, but the salesman is selling a "rarey," a small, cute furry animal that barely eats anything and requires little care.

The woman is smitten and immediately buys it.

She quickly finds that despite only eating a tiny bit of food, her pet grows fast and quite large, soon covering the whole table, then the backyard. The government is called in, and they bring in engineers who say the only way to destroy the creature is to push it off the edge of the Grand Canyon.

They get the creature there using a fleet of trucks and use a lever to tip it off the side, and the creature looks down and says, "It's a long way to tip a rarey..."

In the 2000s, Mercedes ran a commercial featuring a barbershop quartet singing the song as a Mercedes car travels the world. When the car arrives in Tipperary, it turns around and leaves — prompting the singers to be confused and then switch to *"It's a Long way to Sheboygan..."*

Spats (1914)

Spats were a fashion worn by both men and women which came and went several times from the late 1800s until about the 1920s. They are a cloth covering for your shoe, wrapping around the ankle with a strap under the foot to hold it in place. The original, practical usage was to keep mud and dirt from going into your shoes and are still used today in industries where things falling into your shoes — like hot coals — might be a problem.

The following joke likens spats to Chinese foot binding, the ancient (and painful) practice of breaking a young woman's foot bones and binding them to heal in place as a smaller foot. It was considered a sign of status and beauty— but not for everyone, because foot binding was eventually outlawed in China during the early 1900s. I'm assuming this joke was made during a resurgence of the spats fashion in 1914:

> *"You criticize us about foot binding," said the Chinese visitor to the United States, "Yet I see all your women have their feet bound."*
>
> *"That is an epidemic," it was explained to him, "which broke out in 1914. Those are called spats."*

World War I (1914-1918)

World War I was fought in and around Europe and was expected to be "The war to end all wars." After ending it was referred to as "The War" or "The Great War". It wasn't until 1939, when it became obvious that another big war was brewing from the ashes of the previous one that it began to be called "World War I."

The following is a conversation between two private citizens after the war about saving things for the war effort:

> *First Person: Did the War do anything for you?*
>
> *Second Person: Sure did. It taught me to save peach-stones, tin foil,*

newspapers, and all kinds of junk. In fact, I can now save anything except money.

These were all things used to war production. Peach pits "stones" were used to make charcoal for gas masks.

From 1915 to 1916 there was a naval engagement over the Dardanelles, a waterway in Turkey.

Teacher: What lesson do we learn from the attack on the Dardanelles?
Student: That a strait beats three kings.

It's a poker joke: In poker a straight (a hand of cards in rank order) beats three of a kind (a hand with three of the same rank, such as three kings). The "strait" also being Dardanelles (The Strait of Gallipoli, defended by the Ottoman Empire, who won using strategic mines), and the "three kings" being England, France, and Russia.

A librarian said she had a young woman come in who wished to see a large map of France. She was writing a paper on the battlefields of France for a culture club, and she couldn't find Flander's Fields or No Man's Land on any of the maps in her books.

The young woman here is mixing up military terminology for place names. "Flander's Fields" is the name of an unspecific area consisting of multiple battlefields in Belgium. It was popularized in a famous 1915 poem called *In Flanders Fields*. "No Man's Land" is a military term for any disputed, dangerous area between battlefronts in war. Also, a "Culture Club" here is an extracurricular school activity learning about different cultures, and not the 1981 band of the same name.

It's a modern joke, but in the TV series Doctor Who, the titular time traveler meets a soldier from The Great War and has a slip of the tongue in terminology, leading the soldier to ask:

> *Soldier: Yes, but, what do you mean, "World War One"?*

Coal Shortage in New York (1917-1918)

Coal was commonly used for heat before being replaced by electric and gas in the 1960s. The winter of 1917-1918 was particularly brutal in New York City, and coal was scarce between demand and its need during the war. This joke references that shortage, but it's a double entendre.

> *During the recent coal shortage, when the population of New York had its fuel rationed, a coal dealer sent one of his truckmen with a load of hard and soft coal up to his house in the suburbs, with instructions to dump both loads in his cellar, in different corners. The coal man's wife was glad to receive the coal, but after he*

had finished loading the soft into the cellar she was suddenly called away to town and locked her house.

The truckman, unable to release the rest of the coal, wired his employer as follows: "Dropped one load. Got my hard on. She has it closed so I can't put it in!"

United States Prohibition (1920-1934)

The Temperance movement eventually succeeded in making the consumption of alcohol for non-medicinal purposes illegal in the United States with a constitutional amendment in 1919. This backfired and led to a rise in organized crime. The amendment was repealed 14 years later, in 1933.

Once, during Prohibition, I was forced to live for days on nothing but food and water.[1]

This jokes that alcohol is a necessity, not a luxury.

Even casual drinkers were now criminals forced to hide their drinking.

During prohibition, a man goes to the tailor and asks for a pocket to be sewn into his jacket. The tailor asks, "Pint or quart?"

---

[1] W.C. Fields

As in "how big is the bottle you want to hide in your jacket?"

Farmer: Would you like to buy a jug of cider?
Man: Well... uh... is it ambitious and willing to work?

Hard work, hard cider. In other words, "Is it 'hard' cider"?

"Where can you get alcohol?" was a whispered question asked by many.

The wife complained to her husband that the chauffeur was very drunk and must be fired instantly.

"Fired?" the husband retorted joyously. "When he's sobered up, I'll have him take me out and show me where he got it!"

And…

First young woman: Would you marry a man just to reform him?
Second young woman: What's wrong with him?
First young woman: He drinks.
Second young woman: Marry him and find out where he gets it! We need someone like that in our group!

This gives an idea of how people would try to get around the restrictions medically.

Man: Could you write me a prescription for whiskey?
Doctor: Sure, but only if it's justified, such as in the case of rattlesnake bite.
Man: Do you happen to have a rattlesnake, doctor?
Doctor: I most certainly do.
Man: Then please let it bite me, and you can write me a prescription.
Doctor: Let's see... today is May 5th. Come again on September the 16th. Until then all the bites are taken.

This is about a man brought to court for making illegal alcohol.

A man was arraigned with several others for illicit distilling. "Defendant," said the court, "what is your name?"

"Joshua," was the reply.

"Are you the man who made the sun stand still?"

Quick as a flash came the answer: "No, sir; I am the man who made the moonshine."

It refers to the biblical story of Joshua, who stopped the sun for more time to defeat his enemies, and the fact that "moonshine" is a term for any illegally made alcohol.

"Dry" meant supporting prohibition, and "wet" meant supporting its repeal. Former New York State Governor Al Smith sought the Democratic 1928 and 1932 presidential nominations, losing the primaries first to Herbert Hoover and then to Franklin Delano Roosevelt. Smith's support for the repeal of prohibition is the basis for this joke, playing on the term "wet."

> *Gentlemen, it is our pleasure to announce to you that Mr. Al Smith has accepted the nomination as Democratic candidate for the President of the United States. We have no doubt he will pull the votes of the country's entire male population. We are planning an extensive campaign, and every State will in a few days be flooded with the slogan:*
>
> *VOTE FOR AL SMITH*
> *AND HAVE YOUR*
> *WET DREAMS COME TRUE*

A "wet dream" is a term for a very sexual dream.

Chief Justice William Howard Taft (1921-1930)

William Howard Taft was the 27th President of the United States. He was also overweight, and there is a myth that he became stuck in the White House bathtub. There are many fat jokes about him, but they are largely recycled material that could be about anyone.

> *Taft was so fat, he sat in two branches of the federal government.*

This a play on the truth— he was President of the United States (1909-1913) and then served as Chief Justice of the Supreme Court, but it was not simultaneously, as the joke implies.

The Hall-Mills Murder Case (1922)

Edward Wheeler Hall, an Episcopal priest; and Eleanor Mills, a choir member he allegedly was having an affair with[1], were found murdered on September 14, 1922.

> *Soon after the Hall-Mills murder case the Methodist Episcopal College of New Jersey met and passed a ruling that hereafter all rectors must button their collars in front, and their pants behind!* [2]

Supposedly this was to keep them from cheating on their wives, switching where the collars and pants are fastened. No such thing was actually done; it was just a joke about keeping clergy from fooling around.

---

[1] The murderer was never found.

[2] Will Rogers

Events: 1925-1950

Wall Street Crash (1929)

In October 1929, the New York Stock Exchange dropped quickly, leading to the Great Depression. People were losing their entire fortunes. The worst day was Black Thursday— October 24. A rumor took shape that there were mass suicides jumping out windows. This did not actually happen, but humorists and cartoonists picked it up and ran with it.

> *The strangest weather phenomenon was in 1929, when it started raining investors.*

And a more modern take on it, referring to the September 11, 2001, terrorist attacks:

> *A time traveler lands in New York and emerges from his machine to find chaos, and men falling from a building, bodies on the ground.*
>
> *"Oh my god," he exclaims. "It's September 11, 2001!"*
>
> *A man next to him replies "No, it's October 24th, 1929."*

Because of Black Thursday, financial markets have systems built in to stop trading if things start to get too far out of hand, giving traders a chance to breathe and think.

The Great Depression (1929-1939)

The newly-built Empire State Building— then the tallest building in the world— was completed in 1931 and remained 75% vacant during most of the 1930s due to the Great Depression. This led to a local name for it:

The Empty State Building

Due to the poor economy of the great depression, people occasionally put buttons into the church collection plate so it seemed they were giving to the church as the collection plate was passed. Coins may not seem like much of a donation today, but a quarter in 1935 equals $6 buying power in 2025

Usher: Things are definitely improving for the congregation.
Minister: What makes you say that?
Usher: We're getting better quality buttons in the collection plate.

This one describes a fictional contraption where you would make less noise the more money you put in.

The pastor announced to the congregation that the church would today use a new automatic collection basket.

He said, "If you put in a half-dollar or a quarter, it will fall silently onto a cushion. If you put in a nickel, a bell will ring, and if you drop in a button, a pistol will go off."

The pistol mentioned here I'm assuming just represents a loud noise, though the idea of cheating parishioners actually being shot is another, rougher interpretation.

Reno Divorce (1931)

Before the 20th century, highly restrictive laws meant getting a divorce in America was no small task. This changed most notably in 1931, when the city of Reno, Nevada reduced the residency requirement to six weeks and allowed wider grounds for divorce. Reno also did not require both parties to be present in court. This was helpful for couples who wanted to separate amicably— the husband could stay in the home state and work while the wife moved to Reno and fulfilled the residency requirement— and for people whose spouse had run off or was missing. Reno became the "Divorce Capital of the World" and retained the title until the late 1960's when other states and municipalities relaxed their laws.

This next joke is not outdated, but sets up the outdated joke:

First Person: Where was the Declaration of Independence signed?
Second Person: Philadelphia.
First person: No, at the bottom of the page!

The humor is in mixing up the locality where it was signed and the location on the document where it was signed.

The following joke is an alternate punchline, where the second person upsets the expectation.

First Person: Where was the Declaration of Independence signed?
Second Person: Reno!

In a divorce you declare yourself to be independent of your former spouse.

The Hague, a city in the Netherlands, is home to many international and European judicial organizations, famously hosting two international law conventions in 1899 and 1907 that laid down rules for warfare and establishing war crimes. Swap the genders here as you wish, it works both ways:

Wife [Trying to think of The Hague]: What is the name of the place where so much was done toward promoting peace in the world?
Husband: Reno, my dear.

And…

Q: Why did the woman go to Nevada?
A: To be Reno-vated.

A pun off "renovated."

King Edward VIII (1936)

King Edward VIII of England abdicated the throne in 1936 to eventually marry an American woman (Wallis Simpson), who was in the process of getting her second divorce.

Edward went from being Admiral of the Fleet to third mate on an American tramp.

As King, Edward held the title "Admiral of the Fleet," outranking all military officers. "Third mate" is the fourth in charge on a ship, and third spouse. A "tramp" is both a term for a loose woman and a "tramp steamer," which is a cargo ship that doesn't follow a fixed delivery schedule, it simply picks up and drops off loads whenever and wherever it can.

World War II (1939-1945)

World War II was waged over a large area – a truly global conflict - encompassing Europe, Northern Africa, and the Pacific Ocean.

It was a very ugly war, and the warnings previously given regarding language and content from the introduction strongly apply in this section.

World War II: Adolph Hitler

Adolph Hitler rose to power in Germany and is viewed as the instigator behind the evils of World War II. This joke dates to before the invasion of France in 1940.

> *Q: Who is the world's most perverse, diseased, living man?*
> *A: Adolph Hitler. He fucked his way into power; browned all the German youth; fucked the Jews out of their possessions; clap-ped them in jail; syph-ted the literature of the country; has the scum of Germany behind him and now he wants to lick the hole of France.*

The above is full of references to Hitler's rise to power.

- "Fucked his way into power," Hitler's rise involved unethical activities like coercion and threats.
- "Browned all the German youth," the *Sturmabteilung,* (literally, "Storm Division" or "Storm Troopers"), the paramilitary force of the Nazi Party, wore brown uniform shirts[1], here and refers to feces.
- "Fucked the Jews out of their possessions," Hitler was blaming the Jews for all the problems in Germany, taking their wealth to fund the war effort.

---

[1] Literally called "Braunhemden" the "brown shirts"

- This next section alludes to sexually transmitted diseases (STDs) twice; clap-ped them in jail; syph-ted the literature of the country" refers to gonorrhea and syphilis and then to burning books which were considered subversive.
- "He wants to lick the hole of France" to "lick" someone is defeat them, and to lick with a tongue, and a pun off "hole" meaning asshole and "whole" meaning the entire country.

In 1939, a song regarding the testicles (and implied manliness) of the leaders of the Nazi Party popped up among British soldiers, original author unknown still. It's sung to the tune of the World War I tune, "The Colonel Bogey March," which later became better known as "The River Kwai March" after it was used in the 1957 movie *The Bridge on the River Kwai*.

It goes:

Hitler has only got one ball,
Göring has two but very small,
Himmler has something sim'lar,
But poor old "Go-balls" has no balls at all.

This refers to four men at the top of German leadership: Adolf Hitler, Hermann Göring, Heinrich Himmler, and Joseph Goebbels.[1]

I have a family story about this. Supposedly my grandfather had been singing the song to himself around

[1] "Goebbels" is pronounced "go-bulls" which was intentionally mispronounced as "go-balls" in the tune.

the house one day in the early 1950s but only humming "ball" and "no balls" because there were children present. That evening, as he was having a beer with a friend, my young mother came up to him and asked, "Daddy, what does Hitler only have one of?" My grandfather was caught so off-guard he spit out his beer.

World War II: French Surrender

Nazi Germany hit France hard and fast in May 1940, forcing the French to surrender in only a month and a half. Germany had France outclassed and beaten, but that didn't mean the rest of the world didn't poke a little dark-humor fun at France for giving up too quickly.

> *Q: How many Frenchmen does it take to defend Paris?*
> *A: We don't know, they've never tried.*

And…

> *Q: Why are there trees along the Champs-Elysees?*
> *A: So the Nazis could walk in the shade.*

The Champs-Elysees is a famous street in Paris, and implies the French put the trees there for the comfort of any invaders.

A fake ad in a newspaper:

French rifle for sale: Never fired, dropped once.

When you surrender, you generally put both hands up in the air to show you are unarmed and don't pose a threat.

If you're British, raise your hand. If you're French, raise two hands.

The Statue of Liberty was a gift to America from France in 1886:

If France had a Statue of Liberty, it would have both hands up.

World War II: The Holocaust

Nazi Germany committed the worst known genocide in history during World War II, killing six million Jews in concentration camps and burning the bodies. The Jews had been discriminated against for many years beforehand and were practically a ready-made scapegoat for the Nazi Party to blame for anything. The wealth seized from the Jewish population partially funded their war.

Jewish oppression was nothing new in Europe, but during Hitler's rise, it increased. This joke was made in the late 1930's when people knew that Hitler didn't like Jews, but before the holocaust actually started.

Since Adolph Hitler has come into power a new type of circumcision has become the vogue in Germany. The rabbi snips off the foreskin, saves it, and throws the Jew away.

This reverses the Jewish ceremony of *Brit Milah,* when the foreskin of an infant boy's penis is removed on the eighth day after birth.

In 1939, Jews were required to wear a yellow Star of David to show that they were Jewish.

A person was walking down the street in the Jewish Ghetto with a large Star of David on their chest.

A Nazi guard yells out, "Hey, are you a Jew?"

They pointed to the star on their chest and said, "What do you think I am, a fucking sheriff?"

Sherriff badges are stars. This humor is in that it would be near suicidal for a Jew to respond that way.

This is a "fake-out joke" told when someone tells a holocaust joke - and you haven't yet, or it will be obvious what you're doing.

[someone tells a holocaust joke]
"That's terrible! My grandfather died in a concentration camp!"
[let that sink in for a moment then continue]

> *"…he got drunk and fell off the guard tower."*

That plays off the fact that the immediate reaction from group members will be sympathy or shame, then you play off the fact that even though the fictional grandfather "died in a concentration camp" he was actually a guard, drunk on duty, and thus probably deserved to die anyway.

Some German citizens kept Jews hidden and/or safe from the Nazis as long as they could. That's the setup for this one:

> *A man goes to confession and confesses about keeping a Jewish woman hidden in his house, safe from Nazis. The priest says that's something to be proud of, and not a sin.*
>
> *The man says that sometimes she would get lonely and have sex with him. The priest says that is understandable, and forgivable— after all he saved her life! Hardly worth confessing or needing forgiveness for.*
>
> *"Well," says the young man finally, "Do I have to tell her the war is over?"*

The man doesn't want to set her free because he wants to continue getting the free sex.

The following joke takes place after the war and refers to the fact that Jews in the Auschwitz concentration camp were tattooed with numbers for identification.

An old man wins big in the lottery. He goes to the synagogue, gives them a million dollars. His friends say, "What a nice guy!"

He goes down to the local deli and gives a million dollars to the old guy who runs the slicer. His friends say, "What a nice guy!"

He gets on a plane, flies to Germany, and gives a million dollars to the German government. He comes back and his friends say "WHAT? You gave a million dollars to Germany, after all the hell they put you through?"

He points to his tattoo and says, "Where do you think I got the numbers?"

I've seen people tell this joke and pull down their lower lip as the say the punchline as if the Jews were tattooed there, because that's how they themselves heard it. If you tell it that way it's fine, but from a historical perspective the tattoos were on the arm. If you want to use a gesture and point out where the tattoo was in the correct place, it was on the back of the right arm, between the elbow and the back of the hand.

World War II: Soldiers

Southern England, especially London, was hit hard. Civilian casualties were high, while actual military casualties were low because they were on guard duty or training elsewhere.

That brought on a joke about enlisting:

Join the Army and miss the war!

This next one is about the busy work that soldiers were given to keep them occupied. You can imagine that with how prevalent smoking was - cigarettes were even included in their daily rations - it was a common "busy work" chore to pick up the discarded cigarette butts off the ground.

As I remember it, we had four enemies—
Japan, Germany, Italy, and cigarette butts—
not necessarily in that order.

This is about how soldiers are supposed talk to the locals in North Africa:

A Texas sergeant addressed his troops upon landing in Africa.

He said "We want to get along with the locals, so don't argue with them. For instance, if they say Africa is bigger than Texas, just agree and move on."

Africa is 45 times larger than Texas, but Texas was the largest US state and was very proud of that until much-larger Alaska was admitted to the United States in 1959.

World War II: Kamikaze Attacks

Computer-guided weaponry did not exist in the 1940s. The Japanese employed Kamikaze pilots who would die by intentionally crashing their planes into targets.

> *Too bad about kamikaze pilots. They had to do all their bragging ahead of time.*

And this next one plays off "it's just plain suicide" and "suicide by plane."

> *I don't know why they call it "kamikaze," I mean, it's just "plane suicide."*

And...

> *Q: What's the prerequisite for becoming a kamikaze pilot?*
> *A: A fear of ejection.*

It's a play on "fear of rejection." Aircraft ejection seats— which blast a pilot (somewhat) safely clear of an airplane in trouble— were still being developed by the Allies during World War II. The Japanese didn't have them at all.

Here's a math World War II joke:

> *Q: How do you divide by Zero?*
> *A: By becoming a kamikaze and splitting a ship in half.*

In mathematics, division by zero is simply called "undefined" and stops with an error message because if allowed the calculator would never stop the division operation. The punchline here doesn't require you knowing more mathematics than that - a "Mitsubishi A6M Zero" was a Japanese-made aircraft commonly used by Kamikaze pilots. Now if one Zero could actually split a ship in half is up to discussion, but it's still an unexpected math joke in World War II humor.

World War II: D-Day

The Invasion of Normandy was named "Operation Overlord" and took place on June 6, 1944. Most people call it "D-Day" which is a general military term used for when an attack is supposed to happen.

It was the largest invasion from the sea in history, involving thousands of ships and watercraft. There's an urban legend (though many people claim it's a true story), about a German coast guardsman sighting the invasion and contacting his superiors.

German soldier: Ships on the channel!
German commander: How many ships?
German soldier: All of them!

Post World War II

Chad (also called Kilroy) was a common hand-drawn meme character in World War II. This often was paired with the saying "Wot, no ____?" (meaning "What, no

____?") and referring to various items rationed during the war such as "Wot, no coffee?" "Wot, no sugar?" etc. After the end of the war, of course this included something that was not rationed but now, thankfully, unavailable:

Wot, no Fuhrer?

Referring to "Der Fuhrer," Adolf Hitler.

For this one it's now impossible to find someone who had a grandfather who could say that they did this during World War II:

> *A grandfather yelled at his grandson. "You kids today are wimps! When I was your age I went to Paris, I got drunk, danced with the ladies, I pissed on a bartender and got into a fight!"*
>
> *The youth was determined to show his grandfather he wasn't a wimp, but a few days later the grandfather noticed his grandson had a black eye. "What happened to you?" the grandfather asked.*
>
> *"I did what you said, grandfather! I went to Paris, got drunk, danced with the ladies, pissed on a bartender... and then I got beaten up!"*
>
> *"Well, who did you go with?" the grandfather asked.*
>
> *"Just some friends, grandfather. ...Who did you go with?"*
>
> *"Oh, the 7th Panzer division."*

The grandfather was a German invader, so of course he could do whatever he wanted.

This one plays with the names of airplane manufacturers.

> *An old pilot who had served in the Royal Air Force during World War II was relating the events to a classroom full of children. He said, "So, there were four Fokkers on the horizon - "*
>
> *The children giggle wildly at this, and the teacher hurriedly interrupts and explains to the children, "'Fokker' was a type of aircraft."*
>
> *The old pilot says, "That's true, but these Fokkers were Messerschmitts."*

Fokker was an airplane manufacturer founded by the Dutch aviator Anthony Fokker, and supplied aircraft to Germany during World War I. The joke plays off "Fokkers" sounding like "fuckers" - which it turned out really was the old man's intended word. "Messerschmitt" was the primary manufacturer of German airplanes during World War II.

After the end of World War II, some surviving German pilots - who had bombed London many times - unsurprisingly became commercial airline pilots, leading to this joke. Lufthansa is Germany's national airline:

I love taking Lufthansa back to London—
the pilots always know the way. [1]

Lucky Strike's cigarette packaging was green with gold stripes. During World War II the materials to make those color dyes (chromium and copper), were in short supply so they switched to a white package and started an ad campaign in 1942 explaining the change as: "Lucky Strike Green has gone to war!"

The old green package was never brought back. This led to people making this rhetorical question for years afterwards when they saw the white package:

Do you think Lucky Strike Green will ever
come back from the war?

In 1992, 47 years after the end of World War II, a Disneyworld resort opened outside of Paris, France. The "French surrender" joke came back to life with:

Q: Did you hear about the trouble the first
day Disneyland Paris opened?
A: When the fireworks went off the first
night, everyone living nearby ran
outside and surrendered.

The Cold War (1947-1991)

The Cold War was a 44-year standoff between the Soviet Union and the United States of America, starting in

---

[1] Attributed to John Lennon

the aftermath of World War II and lasting until the fall of the Soviet Union in 1991. The term "Cold War" was coined by George Orwell and was "cold" because both sides had large militaries they would brag about, but in the end neither really used.

No one should have been surprised by the rise of the Soviet Union after World War II. I mean, there were red flags everywhere.

A "red flag" is a term for a warning, and the Soviet flag was red with a yellow star and a hammer and sickle.

After World War II Europe was divided between the western allies and the eastern allies from the war. Germany itself was split into two sections— the Democratic West and the Socialist East. Rubella was first identified by German scientists in 1814, leading to the popular name "German measles."

I had German measles. The doc gave me two shots— one for East, and one for West!

East and West Germany reunified in 1991, after the Cold War ended.

In this one the humor is the general doesn't know the range of the bomber… except for how long it takes to bomb Moscow.

A newspaper reporter was asking a general about the Air Force's new bomber. He asked how long it would take to fly from

New York to Paris. The General didn't know.

He asked how long it would take for it to fly from San Francisco to Honolulu. Again, the general said he didn't know.

Finally, he asked how long it would take to fly from New York to Moscow. Without hesitation, the General said, "7 hours, 29 minutes, and 14 seconds."

After the 1950s, the idea of putting nuclear bombs in easy-to-shoot-down bombers was dropped in favor of putting nuclear warheads on Inter-Continental Ballistic Missiles (ICBMs), leading to this "the Post Office is slow" joke:

It's discouraging that the Russians have something that can get to every American city in 30 minutes, while the Post Office doesn't.

Harry Truman (1948)

Harry Truman was the Vice President of the United States in 1945 when President Franklin Delano Roosevelt died, leaving Truman as President. When he ran for reelection in 1948, he won against Thomas Dewey, who was ahead in the polls. Some people were so certain Dewey would win that the Chicago Daily Tribune jumped the gun and printed papers with the headline "Dewey Defeats Truman," and there is a famous photograph (actually several, from different angles) of Truman holding up the incorrect paper aloft for all to see. I point this out because it's now so far in the past that people seeing the picture and not knowing the context might assume that the man holding the paper is Dewey, not Truman - the picture itself is a dated joke for that reason.

In this next joke you need to understand that Gallup is a company famous for conducting public opinion polls.

> *Harry Truman is the first president to lose*
> *in a Gallup and win in a walk.*

Here making a pun of "Gallup" the poll, and "to gallop" like a horse running. Generally galloping is faster than walking, hence the joke.

Some Enchanted Evening (1949)

"Some Enchanted Evening" is a song from the 1949 Rogers and Hammerstein Musical *South Pacific*.

> *Knock-knock!*
> *Who's there?*
> *Sam and Janet.*
> *Sam and Janet who?*
> *"Sam and Janet evening..."*

It's a pun on the title and first line of the song.

Events: 1950-1975

Rock Music (1950s)

Instruments like guitars and basses were being electrified and advancements had been made in sound amplification by the 1930s, but World War II rationing made introducing any new electronic technology to musicians difficult until after the war in 1945.

By the 1950s, bands using the new instruments became popular as Rock and Roll took off.

> *I'm fascinated by these rock groups who have all the electrical equipment on stage. I know a musician who doubles— he plays first guitar and second fuse box.*

Of course no one plays "fuse box", but I guess technically that is what the road crew does.

It really was a change from the big band era to Rock and Roll, so here's a few jokes about "I don't like the kid's music these days" from that time.

This one is standard "old people complaining about new music," implying that the expensive equipment comes at the expense of talent.

> *People wonder how rock groups can afford all that expensive equipment but think about the money they save on music lessons.*

And…

Show me an adult who can smile at a rock and roll concert, and I'll show you a hearing aid with weak batteries.

Folk music went through a revival starting in the 1940s then peaking in the 1960s, using the new electrified instruments.

A folk singer is a person who sings about the joys of a simple life— using a $5,000 sound system.

Youth Subculture (1950s-1970s)

After World War II there was marked disconnect between teenagers, young adults, and their parents, particularly 1950-1970, and relaxing a bit when that generation had children of its own.

During that phase of life, teens and young adults are always a little rebellious, but it was more pronounced in this era with the new changes in society and technology. Marriage was being put off until after college. Cars were giving young people more independence; ideas and fashions were freely and quickly passed on by radio and television.

Many of the parents of this generation either served in or watched World War II as it happened. This joke plays off the German word for submarine "Unterseeboot" (undersea boat), which was anglicized to "U-Boat."

My daughter said she was going to join the subculture. I said, "forget it! No kid of mine is going to work on a U-Boat!"

A common way for young men to rebel was to grow their hair long and stop shaving.

There's something unnerving about a kid with a Daniel Boone Haircut, a Mark Twain moustache, and an Abraham Lincoln beard telling me he is "rejecting the past."

The actual "past" the youth was rejecting was that of their parents, but not as far back as the 1800s.

This follows the assumption that if a young man grew his hair long, he must not care about keeping themselves clean:

It used to be if you asked what has long hair, smells bad, and follows your daughter around, the answer would be "the dog," but now it's "her boyfriend"!

A barbershop quartet is a group of singers of a specific style from the late 1800s and early 1900s, the origins as shaky, but a barber shop was a community center, and this type of singing was named after it.

I went to a rock group, and I told them "You fellas really have good voices. You could be a great barbershop quartet!"

They asked, "What's that?"
I said, "What, a quartet?"
They replied "No, what's a barbershop?"

Drugs were famously experimented with by youth through this period, leading to this joke starting in the 1970s:

If you remember the 1960s, you weren't there.

Implying that everyone during the 1960s was high on drugs and therefore wouldn't recall the events.

A term for youth following the counterculture in the 1960s was "hippy." This joke is a play on that, and the way that some people count of seconds by saying "One Mississippi, two Mississippi…"

Q: How does a 1960s polygamist count his wives?
A: One Mrs. Hippy, two Mrs. Hippy, three Mrs. Hippy...

The Space Race (1950-1969)

The Space Race was between the United States of America and the Soviet Union from the 1950s to the 1970s.

The United States had a string of flubbed public rocket launches, leading to this joke:

Q: How can you tell the children of rocket scientists from the other children?
A: Instead of counting one to ten, they count: "10, 9, 8, 7, 6, 5, 4, 3, 2, 1 - SHIT!"

Because that's how rocket scientists counted during a failed launch.

Werner Von Braun was a German rocket scientist in World War II, where he helped design the V-2 rocket, which was used to reach targets in Europe and England from 200 miles away. After the war he and other German scientists were moved to the United States and worked on the space program there— the Soviet Union did the same for their own space program. A movie was made about him in 1960, titled *I Aim at the Stars: the Werner von Braun story* which led to a joke title that long outlasted the film, saying that instead the film's title should have been:

I aim at the stars: sometimes I hit London. [1]

This next joke refers to the German scientists working on both sides.

During the Cold War, the US and the USSR each launched satellites that passed each other now and then.

When they pass each other over the United States, the American satellite says, [speaking like a cowboy] "Howdy partner,

[1] Mort Sahl

how are ya?" and the Russian satellite replies "Very well, thank you!"

When they pass each other over Russia, the Russian satellite starts with "Dobre denjee, tovarich!" [Good day, comrade!] and the American satellite replies in kind.

When they pass each other at night, behind the earth, they whisper "Guten tag! Wenn wir jetzt hinter der Erde sind, koennen wir gut alle Deutcsch spechen, ja?" [Good day! When we're behind the Earth we can speak German, right?]

Manifest Destiny was the 19th-century belief that the United States was destined to expand all the way across North America to the Pacific Ocean. It was eventually realized, but at the expense of the Native Americans who were already living there.

When NASA was preparing for the Apollo project, they did some astronaut training on a Navajo reservation. One day, a Navajo elder and his son were herding sheep and came across the NASA crew. The old elder, who only spoke Navajo, asked a question which the son translated, "What are the guys in the big suits doing?"

A member of the crew said they were practicing for their trip to the moon. The old elder got excited and asked through his son if he could send a message to the moon with the astronauts. Recognizing a promotional opportunity for the space program, the NASA crew found a tape recorder and let the elder record a message in Navajo.

After the old man recorded his message, they asked his son to translate the message. The son refused. The NASA representatives brought the tape to the reservation, where the rest of the tribe listened and laughed, but refused to translate the elder's message to the moon for the representatives.

Finally, NASA called in an official government translator. He reported that the message for the moon said: "Watch out for these guys; they've come to steal your land."

The elder was trying to warn ahead to any potential beings living there how the United States treats natives.

The Vietnam War (1955-1975)

The Vietnam War was between North and South Vietnam but was also a "proxy war" between the Soviet Union and the United States.

Many in the United States didn't feel Vietnam was a war worth fighting in, and when a draft was enacted, many Americans fled to Canada because Canada did not officially participate in the Vietnam War.

When people ask me what brought my family to Canada, I just tell them my dad was stationed here during the Vietnam war.

Implying his father wasn't stationed there, he went there to flee the United States draft.

When I joined the Army, the Selective Service wasn't very selective. My draft notice was addressed to "occupant."

"Occupant" is used in postal mail product advertising sent out to an entire neighborhood, when the advertising company doesn't know the name of the persons living in the house.

Many Americans point out the fact that the United States didn't lose but "pulled out of the conflict," but yep, they lost. They had some victories but had a hard time fighting a prolonged guerrilla war against a low-technology opponent... which is the basis for this next joke.

An Englishman and an American are talking about war and which of their countries is the strongest. The American thinks of the American Revolution against England as his winning argument and simply says, "How can the world's strongest army lose to people with farm equipment and inferior weaponry?"

The Englishman is taking his time thinking, and after some time answers,

"We're talking about the Vietnam War, right?"

The Englishman is pointing out that America lost in Vietnam for the same reasons they won their Revolutionary War.

My grandfather survived Agent Orange during the Vietnam war. My great grandfather survived mustard gas in World War I. I come from a line of seasoned veterans.

"Seasoning" can mean either flavoring or experience. Agent Orange is an herbicide (weedkiller) used by the United States to clear jungle spaces in Vietnam. Agent Orange was subsequently linked to multiple cancers in soldiers and civilians, resulting in lawsuits. Mustard gas is a chemical warfare agent used in World War I.

Alaska (1959)

Texas was the largest US state upon its admission to the Union in 1845. Texans made a big deal about this — and still do, at least about being big.

Alaska was admitted to the Union in 1959, and is 2.5 times larger than Texas, leading to the following joke:

Alaska was so tired of Texas grumbling about becoming the second largest state and threatened to split itself evenly into two states… so Texas would be the third largest state instead.

The Twist (1959)

The Twist was a song and dance craze starting in 1959.

A young man goes to pick up his date, and while waiting for her to come downstairs the girl's father suggests "You should take my daughter out and screw. She loves it! As a matter of fact, my daughter spent all last night screwing!"

The young man is quite understandably excited by this, and when his date comes downstairs, they walk out the door together.

A few minutes later the daughter comes storming back in, screaming. "DAD! It's called 'The TWIST!'"

This joke plays on the fact that you twist something to screw it into something, and the fact that "screwing" is a euphemism for sex.

Mary Poppins (1964)

The musical film *Mary Poppins* has a song about a nonsense word: "Supercalifragilisticexpialidocious." A pun on that nonsense word is the punchline to this joke.

Mahatma Gandhi walked barefoot most of the time, which produced an impressive set of calluses on his feet. He also ate very little, which made him rather frail, and, with his odd diet, he suffered from bad breath.

This made him a "super calloused fragile mystic vexed by halitosis."

Rose Kennedy (1968)

Rose Kennedy was the matriarch of the politically active Kennedy family. She lost several of her high-profile children: Son Joseph P. Kennedy, Jr in action in World War II, daughter Kathleen Kennedy Cavendish died in a plane crash in 1948, son President John F. Kennedy was assassinated in Dallas, Texas in 1963, and son Senator Robert F. Kennedy was assassinated in Los Angeles in 1968.

The joke involving her is a rhetorical question of the sort people say when their answer to a question is emphatically yes, such as "Is the Pope Catholic?" (Yes, he's the head of the Catholic Church) or "Does a bear shit in the woods?" (Yes, because they live in the woods.)

Along the same lines as that is:

Does Rose Kennedy own a black dress?

Absolutely, considering the number of public family funerals she had to attend, and time spent in mourning.

Landing on the Moon (1969)

The United States landed on the moon six times between 1969 and 1972, ending the Space Race. People have been claiming that the moon landings were faked since they happened. Stanley Kubrick directed the movie *2001: A Space Odyssey* in 1968 which won an Academy Award for Best Special Visual Effects, inspiring many moon landing deniers to claim he had directed the staging of the moon landing.

> *Q: Did you hear about when NASA hired director Stanley Kubrick to fake the moon landing?*
> *A: Unfortunately for them, he was such a perfectionist he forced them to let him shoot on location.*

The joke implies Kubrick forced them to go to the moon anyway to "fake" the moon landing.

Edward "Teddy" Kennedy and Chappaquiddick (1969)

Teddy Kennedy (1932-2009) was a senator from Massachusetts famously involved in the "Chappaquiddick Incident." He was driving a car on Chappaquiddick Island with Mary Jo Kopechne, a congressional intern, in the passenger seat. He drove off a bridge and was able to swim to safety, but Kopechne, unable to get out of the submerged car, drowned. He was in a daze for some time and didn't report the incident to police until hours later. Debate continues to this day whether he was having an affair with Kopechne, was actually dazed, or was simply concerned about his political career.

> *"If Ted Kennedy is such a gentleman, why does it take him nine hours to open a girl's car door?"* [1]

There was a drinking song sung about him, the "Teddy Kennedy Song" in the late 1970s. Sung to the tune of "The Irish Washerwoman" it goes like this:

> *Oh, your mother is old,*
> *And your father is dead,*
> *And your brother is dead,*
> *And your brother is dead,*
> *And your brother is dead,*
> *And your kid has one leg,*
> *And your wife is a drunk,*
> *And your car doesn't float.*
> *[Optional at the end:]*
> *...and your girlfriend can't swim!*

To clarify:

- His mother, Rose Kennedy, was in her late 80s.
- His father, Joseph Kennedy, Sr., passed away a few months after the Chappaquiddick incident.
- Brother Joseph P. Kennedy, Jr. died in action during World War II in 1944.

[1] Dennis Miller

- Brother President John F. Kennedy was assassinated in 1963.
- Brother Senator Robert F. Kennedy was assassinated in 1968.
- His son, Edward M. Kennedy, Jr. had a cancer in his leg in 1974, resulting in it being amputated— he eventually made a full recovery and went on to become a senator for the state of Connecticut.
- His wife, Joan Bennett Kennedy, had a very public drinking problem.
- The "and my girlfriend can't swim" part refers to Mary Jo Kopechne, and is sung the same way as the "*...and many more*" traditionally sung after singing "Happy Birthday to You."

Ford Pinto (1970)

The Ford Pinto was a subcompact car made between 1970 and 1980. It had a glaring flaw in that the gas tank was located right behind the rear bumper. Several rear-end collisions resulted in fire and death.

> *My wife is like a Ford Pinto. She always blows up when I try to ram her in the ass.*

The reference is comparing the Ford Pinto to his wife's anger at him when unexpectedly trying anal sex.

Wings (1971)

After The Beatles broke up, Paul McCartney formed a band named Wings with his wife, Linda. Some people felt Linda lacked talent, and some were probably just jealous she was "the girl who got to marry Paul McCartney" and not them. There was a joke playing off this:

> *Q: What do you call a pig with wings?*
> *A: Linda McCartney.*

This joke has also been done "dog with wings," and can also be done as a two-parter after "What do you call a horse with wings? A Pegasus…" to further set up the twist in the punchline.

Events: 1975-2000

Cass Elliot and Karen Carpenter (1974 and 1983)

She struggled with her weight and died from a heart attack in 1974 at age 35. However a rumor spread that she had instead choked to death on a ham sandwich. There were many predictable fat jokes about this.

Karen Carpenter, who was half of the brother-sister group The Carpenters, died of heart complications from anorexia in 1983. Despite the nine-year stretch between their deaths, this joke came up:

> *Just think, if Mama Cass had just given that ham sandwich to Karen Carpenter, they'd both be alive today.*

Jonestown (1978)

On November 18, 1978, in Jonestown, Guyana, 909 members of the cult The People's Temple committed suicide by drinking Flavor-Aid laced with poison.

> *Q: Why are there no jokes about the Jonestown Massacre?*
> *A: The punchline is too long.*

"Punch line" being a term for a group of people waiting to use the punch bowl at a party, and "punchline" in a joke.

Anyone who refused the poison was shot and the cult's leader, Jim Jones, committed suicide by gun. An investigative team who had been there were also shot as they tried to leave Jonestown by plane.

Never interrupt someone telling a Jonestown joke. They literally shot people for skipping the punch line.

In March 1997, 39 members of the Heaven's Gate cult were found to have committed suicide in California. It was unrelated to Jonestown, but…

Q: Why did the Heaven's Gate cultists commit suicide?
A: They were keeping up with the Joneses.

A reference to the Jonestown Massacre, and "Keeping up with the Joneses" is a term for "comparing yourself to the neighbors."

Werewolves of London (1978)

Singer-songwriter Warren Zevon's only top 40 hit was "Werewolves of London."

Knock-knock
Who's there?
Ah
Ah who?
Werewolves of London...

The song's refrain is a werewolf howl: "*Ah woo…* werewolves of London." You sing it as if the "Ah who?" was the howl, and you're continuing the line.

The AIDS Epidemic Early Days (1980s)

HIV (Human Immunodeficiency Virus), which leads to AIDS (Acquired Immune Deficiency Syndrome), burst onto the scene in the early 1980s.

Before other methods of transmission were discovered, HIV was originally linked to sex between homosexual men and called GRID for "Gay-Related Immunodeficiency Virus." Homosexuals were a marginalized segment of the population, leading to obvious gay-related jokes.

> *Q: Why haven't they found a cure for AIDS yet?*
> *A: They haven't been able to teach the lab rats to butt fuck.*

And…

> *Q: What does "gay" stand for?*
> *A: Got Aids Yet?*

And referring to gay male sex:

> *Q: What's the first physical sign of AIDS?*
> *A: A sharp pounding in the ass.*

By 1984, it was known that HIV was also transmitted by heterosexuals and contact with infected blood.

From 1983 to 1985 there was a famine in Ethiopia. There were many jokes about this, but they were almost entirely reused "starving person" humor. This one is AIDS-related, though:

Q: What would prevent AIDS from spreading in Africa?
A: Sex only after lunch.

Meaning lunch never happened, so no sex.

Rock Hudson was a Hollywood heartthrob of the 1950s. He had kept his homosexuality private, as was the culture at the time. He was the first celebrity to come out as being HIV positive in July 1985 and died of it three months later. Being the first, he took the brunt of the jokes:

Q: Why did Prudential go out of business?
A: No one wants a piece of "The Rock."

Insurer Prudential Finance's logo is the Rock of Gibraltar, and their slogan was "Get a piece of the rock."

There had been a rumor that Rock Hudson had married actor Jim Nabors in the 1970s— but the truth is they were merely friends, and it doesn't even make sense because gay marriage was illegal everywhere in the 1980s.

Rock Hudson had no friends, but he had Nabors up the ass.

"Nabors" and "Neighbors," and to have something "up the ass" means "a lot."

The Wedding of Prince Charles and Lady Diana (1981)

This relates to Prince Charles's (later King Charles III) first wedding in 1981.

> *Q: Where did Prince Charles spend his honeymoon?*
> *A: Indiana.*

He didn't spend it in the US state of Indiana, it's a sex joke. He married Lady Diana Spencer, (Princess Diana), and thus spent his honeymoon "In Diana."

Natalie Wood (1981)

Actress Natalie Wood drowned while on a weekend boat trip in 1981. It was never learned exactly how she ended up in the water. Two jokes circulated making puns off her last name:

> *Q: What kind of wood doesn't float?*
> *A: Natalie Wood*

And…

> *Q: If you couldn't swim, would you jump off a boat in the middle of the ocean?*
> *A: Well, Natalie would!*

In the second, it's a pun on "Natalie Wood" and "Natalie would."

Def Lepard (1984)

On December 31, 1984, drummer Rick Allen of the rock band Def Lepard lost his arm in an auto accident. He eventually learned to drum with one arm, with the assistance of electronics.

Q: What has ten legs, nine arms and sucks?
A: Def Lepard

Def Lepard has five members, so the math works out.

The Achille Lauro Hijacking (1985)

On October 7, 1985, the PLF (Palestine Liberation Front)— a terrorist group with similar aims to the PLO (Palestine Liberation Organization) — hijacked the passenger ship *Achille Lauro.* The hijackers shot and killed one hostage, a wheelchair-bound Jewish American named Leon Klinghoffer, and pushed his body and wheelchair overboard.

Q: What does PLO stand for?
A: Push Leon Overboard.

Space Shuttle Challenger (1986)

On January 28, 1986, the National Aeronautics and Space Administration's (NASA) Space Shuttle *Challenger* exploded shortly after launch, falling into the ocean and killing all seven astronauts on board.

Q: What does NASA stand for?
A: Need Another Seven Astronauts.

This was reused when the Space Shuttle *Columbia* broke up on reentry in 2003.

The following relates to a soft drink company name (Ocean Spray) and a soft drink name (7-Up):

Q: Did you hear about NASA's new official space drink?
A: Ocean Spray. They couldn't get 7-Up.

Ocean Spray being the splash as it crashed into the ocean, and they couldn't get "seven [people] up" to space.

In 1986, Budweiser introduced a series of television commercials where a patron at a bar would ask for a "light" (meaning a Bud Light) and be given a something with "light," such as a light bulb of some sort.

Q: What were [Challenger astronaut's] last words?
A: I meant a Bud Light!

Because teacher Christa McAuliffe was among the astronauts on board as part of NASA's highly publicized "Teachers in Space" project, schoolchildren across the nation were watching the launch on live television and witnessed the explosion.

Q: What subject did Christa McAuliffe teach?
A: Social Studies, but now she's History.

And:

Q: Did you hear NASA has got a new slogan?
A: Go up a schoolteacher, come down a marine biologist.

Because the wreckage all fell into the ocean.

Post Office Shootings (1986 and 1991)

In two separate incidents, disgruntled United States Post Office employees shot and killed multiple victims in their workplaces. This prompted the term "going postal" to mean "shoot up your workplace."

Q: What does it mean when the flag at the post office is at half-staff?
A: They're hiring.

Flags are lowered to half-staff in a time of mourning, and if they are mourning the loss of workers, they'll need more.

> *"The other day I went to the post office, and I saw they had bulletproof glass. I realized that it wasn't to keep the bullets from going in, it was to keep them from coming out."* [1]

This implies the glass is for the customer's safety.

The Exxon Valdez (1989)

On March 24, 1989, the oil supertanker *Exxon Valdez* grounded on a reef off the coast of Alaska, causing a massive oil spill. Captain Joseph Hazelwood was sleeping off a few drinks in his cabin when this occurred but was sober when he returned to the bridge afterwards to assist in trying to maneuver the ship off of the obstruction. The news falsely reported that he had been intoxicated while he was piloting the ship.

A traditional sea shanty "[What Shall We Do With a] Drunken Sailor" dates back to at least the 1830s. The verses usually list things to make the drunken sailor do for his punishment, but was edited somewhat to go:

> *What shall we do with a drunken sailor? [3x]*
> *Early in the morning?*

---

[1] Louie Anderson

Put him at the wheel of an Exxon Tanker
[3x]
Early in the morning.

Hazelwood was cleared of the charge of drunkenness in court, but the damage to his reputation was done and he was fired from Exxon.

George H. W. Bush (1989-1993)

George H.W. Bush was the 41st President of the United States, with Vice President Dan Quayle. This is a pun on their names.

Q: Why don't they allow dogs in the White House?
A: They chase the quails and piss on the bushes.

This next one was recycled when George H. W.'s son George W. Bush ran successfully for president in 2001.

Q: Why don't Jews want to vote for Bush?
A: Because the last time they listened to a bush they spent 40 years wandering the desert.

This is a reference to the *Book of Exodus* in the Bible, when God speaks to the Hebrews from a burning bush. Later in the book, they are disobedient and wander the desert for 40 years.

The Rodney King Incident (1991)

In March of 1991, Rodney King, a black man, was pulled over by police for drunk driving and speeding and was beaten by four white Los Angeles Police officers. The beating was caught on video camera, one of the first times ordinary citizens recorded an indisputable incident of police brutality, putting the police in the uncomfortable position of being unable to deny the incident or blame it on the victim.

> *The LAPD is changing their motto from "To Protect and Serve."*
>
> *Now it's going to be "We'll Treat You Like a King."*

On April 29. 1992, three of the officers were acquitted (the jury was unable to come to an agreement on the fourth officer). It was a shock to everyone who saw the video of the beating and were certain of a guilty verdict. After a year of racial tension following the case, a week of rioting began in Los Angeles. On May 1, Rodney King made a television appearance, beginning by saying, "I just want to say— you know— can we, can we all get along?" and saying that people needed to work together and calm down. He later sued the city of Los Angeles and was awarded $3.8 million.

Rodney King did have drinking and drug addiction problems he dealt with for the rest of his life.

> *Rodney King got 3.8 million and recently got his fourth DUI... Apparently what he*

*meant to say was "Can't we get a long....
Island Iced Tea?"* [1]

A Long Island Iced Tea is a cocktail, and the joke paraphrases his words during the riots.

Tears in Heaven (1991)

On March 20th, 1991, guitarist Eric Clapton's four-year-old son died when he was left unattended and fell out of the 53rd-floor window of a New York City apartment building. No one was ever found to blame; not knowing there would be children present, a housekeeper hadn't locked the window, and the child's mother assumed the window was locked. Clapton himself was not there when it happened— he was staying at a nearby hotel and was to pick him up later in the day for a day trip. He wrote the song "Tears in Heaven" as a way of coping with the tragedy, and it was a big hit. The popularity of the song and the story of its inspiration of course fostered some jokes.

Q: What's the guitar tuning for "Tears in Heaven"?
A: B A D D A D

The punchline here spells "Bad Dad" in chords. Guitar tuning assigns pitches to the open strings of a guitar and B A D D A D is indeed a possible guitar tuning.

---

[1] Steve Marmel

Q: What's the difference between a toddler and a bag of cocaine?
A: Eric Clapton wouldn't let a bag of cocaine fall out the window.

Clapton did have a drug problem, and this implies he would have taken better care of the drugs than his son.

Paul Reubens (1991)

Paul Reubens was the actor who played Pee-wee Herman on the popular children's show *Pee-wee's Playhouse.* In July of 1991, during a police inspection of an adult movie theater in Florida, he was arrested for indecent exposure.

On *Pee-wee's Playhouse,* many of the objects in the home— windows, chairs, etc.— could talk.

You really can't blame Pee-wee Herman for what he did, I mean it's not like he could just masturbate at home with all his furniture watching him.

Meaning that he had more privacy in the adult theater.

The following joke involves a hand gesture:

Q: What's this? [Hold out your hand and circle your fingers and thumb as if you could hold a penis in it]
A: Pee-wee's Playhouse.

Meaning that's where a penis "pee wee" plays. There's a secondary joke some people made of then opening their hand a little wider (for a bigger penis) for "and this is Pee-wee's dream house".

Credit where credit is due on how to handle being the butt of jokes — this was not the end of Paul Reubens' career. Two months later, he took the stage at the 1991 MTV Video Music Awards in character as Pee-wee Herman, eliciting cheers from the audience.

His first words: "Heard any good jokes lately?"

Waco (1993)

The Branch Davidians were a fringe religious group that started in 1955. From February to April of 1993, the US Government held a siege on their compound in Waco, Texas on suspected weapons and drug violations. The siege ended with a fire starting as they stormed the compound, and 86 members died. Most jokes about this were recycled "people who burned to death" jokes:

> *Q: What does "Waco" stand for?*
> *A: "We Aren't Coming Out!"*

Or…

> *A: "What A Cook-Out!"*

Waco is the name of the nearby Texas town and is not an acronym.

OJ Simpson (1994)

Orenthal James Simpson was a football player, nicknamed "Juice" because his initials "O.J." were the same as the common shorthand for "orange juice." On June 13, 1994 his wife, Nicole Brown Simpson, and her friend Ron Goldman were found stabbed to death, and OJ was an immediate person of interest. However, instead of turning himself in, he ran from police, resulting in a famous public scene of police cars in slow pursuit of OJ's white Ford Bronco SUV. He was taken into custody, and the eight-month long trial was all over the news for years to come. He was acquitted in the end, but his life was checkered after that, and people still debate the case.

The jokes were numerous, with so much material to draw from, not limited to his name, football career, acting career, wealthy lifestyle, and 1990s race issues. The internet was new, and this was probably the first big, popular news event of the Information Age in which jokes could be shared worldwide instantly after creation.

Q: What's the difference between OJ Simpson and the movie Caddyshack?
A: One had a Bronco pursuit and the other had Chevy Chase.

This refers to the 1980 movie Caddyshack, which had the actor Chevy Chase in it, and it also refers to Simpson's run from the police.

The Florida Orange Growers Association has offered to pay all of OJ's legal bills on one condition. He must change his name to "Snapple."

The joke being the makers of orange juice want to be free of the "OJ" connection. Snapple is a brand of drinks.

Q: What is the difference between OJ Simpson and Christopher Reeve?
A: OJ got to walk, Christopher got the chair.

In 1995, actor Christopher Reeve was in a horse-riding accident that left him paralyzed from the neck down. In the criminal system, to "walk" is to be set free of charges, and "get the chair" implies execution in the electric chair—Reeve was in a wheelchair the rest of his life.

These are references to the LA Riots of 1992 after the police from the Rodney King incident were acquitted of using excessive force. The first refers to looking forward to looting and rioting.

I was heartbroken the day OJ Simpson was acquitted. I'd already picked out which TV I wanted.

This one contrasts the reaction to the OJ Verdict with the reaction to the Rodney King verdict.

Remember when OJ Simpson was found innocent and all the white people rioted, looting and damaging property? Oh, that's right, they didn't.

Simpson would end up civilly liable for the deaths in a different trial and would eventually spend time in prison for different crime in the 2000s.

This was a political cartoon near the end of the OJ trial I enjoyed, reflecting on how tired the public was with the whole thing:

A waiter is holding a pitcher out to a diner in a restaurant.
Waiter: More OJ?
Everyone else in the restaurant: NO!!!

Y2K (1999)

Early computers from the 1960s had limited memory capacity. To save memory space, they only used two digits for the year, effectively making them only able to handle a 100 year segment of time before rolling back to 00. This made sense in the 1960s and 1970s when the turn of the century was 30-40 years away, and assuming that the computers would be replaced with new ones by the time the year 2000. Unfortunately, those engineers and programmers had underestimated the old saying "If it ain't broke, don't fix it", and many of these old computers were still in use, even in critical areas such as finance. There was a race to update the computers in time, because computers might start listing the year as 1900, not 2000, potentially leading to conflicts as negative date values appeared. This issue was called “Y2K” for “Year 2000.”

> *Archaeologists have finally discovered the cause of the dark ages— the Y1K problem.*

“Y1K” would be “Year 1000.” The dark ages is an antiquated term for the early middle ages, the 5th to 10th centuries, viewed in retrospect as a time of decline.

In the end, the Y2K computer issue was resolved enough that there were very few issues.

Culture

Adams Express Shipping Company

Adams Express Company was a shipping company started in 1839. Since 1929, it has been an investment company, called Adams Funds.

Q: For what purpose was Eve created?
A: For Adam's Express Company

In the Bible, Adam and Eve were the first people. "Eve was created for the companionship of Adam" is the joke.

Barbershops

Before modern safety razors and electric razors, if you wanted a shave, you had to use a straight edge razor on yourself or go to a barbershop to have a professional do it. Not everyone was as adept at shaving themselves and disposable razors didn't become available until the 20th century. You can still have a barber shave you today, but it's more the full, pampering experience you're paying for, rather than a better shave.

These jokes are about fears of barbers.

Customer: Are you the barber who shaved me before?
Barber: Yes, I am
Customer: Well, chloroform me.

The barber wasn't very good. Chloroform is an inhaled sedative used as an anesthetic.

Customer: May I have a razor, too?
Barber: Why?
Customer: That way it's a fair fight if I have to defend myself.

Then there's this:

A barber had been out drinking the night before and was still obviously recovering at work the next day. When the barber accidentally cut a man's chin, the man looked up and said "You see what comes from hard drinking?"

Yes, sir," replied the barber consolingly, "it makes the skin tender."

The barber had turned it around and made the remark to be about the customer, not himself.

A barber, having been out late the night before, had a shaky hand the next morning and cut a man's cheek four times. After each accident the barber said, as he sponged away the blood: "Oh, dear me, how careless!"

The man took all these gashes in grave silence. But when the shave was over, he filled a glass at the watercooler, took a mouthful of water, and, with compressed lips, proceeded to shake his head from side to side.

"What is the matter?" the barber asked. "You haven't got a toothache, have you?"

"No," said the customer; "I only wanted to see if my mouth would still hold water without leaking."

The following joke comes up again and again in humor books. I don't "get it", but I include it because it's so common. However I can't find any reasonable, verified reason to ask a barber if he has ever "shaved a monkey."

Customer: Did you ever shave a monkey?
Barber: Why, no; but if you sit down, I'll try.

The Barber is calling his customer a monkey.

Beaters (Hunting)

A beater is a person whose job was to scare the game out of bushes for the hunters— it was a dangerous job when doing it with new hunters who had itchy trigger fingers. We get the term "beating about the bush" from this role.

Hunter: I say, are all your beaters out of the wood?
Gamekeeper: Yes, sir.
Hunter: Are you sure?

Gamekeeper: Yes, sir.
Hunter: Have you counted them?
Gamekeeper: No, sir; but I know they're all right.
Hunter: Then I've shot a deer!"

The hunter was making sure he hadn't shot a beater by mistake.

Big Mac Sandwich

This is a joke based on a 1974 McDonalds Restaurant jingle:

> *A new bus driver wanted to impress the students on his new route, so he painted characters from the children's show "Sesame Street" on his bus. At the first stop, he picked up two overweight children, both named "Patty." At the second stop, he picked up a child who was very cool/special, named "Ross." At the third stop, he picked up a child named "Lattice."*
>
> *Partway to school, Ross and the Pattys started to complain because they were playing cards and Lattice was cheating. The driver took Lattice and put the child behind him. Lattice proceeded to take off their shoe and pick at a bunion on their foot.*
>
> *When the bus driver returned to the bus depot, and the other drivers asked how his*

run was he said "Two obese Pattys, special Ross, Lattice cheats, picks his bunions on a Sesame Street bus."

The jingle for the Big Mac Sandwich went "Two all-beef patties, special sauce, lettuce, cheese, pickles, onions, on a sesame seed bun."

Burma-Shave

Burma-Shave was a popular United States brand of shaving cream. It is remembered most for its 1925-1963 advertising gimmick of having a short saying in its advertisements and putting signs – each having one line of the saying at a time - spaced out on the side of the road.

Shave the modern way
No brush
No lather
No rub-in
Big tube 35 cents – Drug stores
Burma-Shave

Eventually some humor was put into the signs, such as:

She kissed the hairbrush
By mistake
She thought it was
Her husband Jake
Burma-Shave

Many were driving-related.

Don't stick your elbow
Out so far
It may go home
In another car
Burma-Shave

And

Johnny drove a motor bike
Ruth was on his knee
He took a bump at 65
And rode on Ruthlessly
Burma-Shave

Those jokes still hit - they're not really outdated. Here's a World War II version which refers to the leaders of the axis countries. Hitler and Hirohito were the leaders of Germany and Japan. "Old Benito" refers to Benito Mussolini, who was executed when trying to escape to Switzerland shortly after Italy fell to the Allies in 1943.

Let's make Hitler
And Hirohito
Feel as bad
as Old Benito
Buy War Bonds
Burma-Shave

That was also an advertisement to buy war bonds – giving the government money it would pay back with interest later to help with the current war effort. The next one is about saving iron for the war effort, and refers to the Japanese:

Slap
The Jap
With
Iron
Scrap
Burma-Shave

Now that you're well aware of the advertising campaign, this outdated joke refers to the final sign in each group. It eventually became a bit of a humorous slam after someone recited any meaningful (or pretentious) piece of poetry, and another person would simply state:

"...Burma-Shave."

Thus bringing the serious poem/saying down to the level of a shaving cream advertisement.

Butcher Shops

Most of the time today you can walk into a grocery store and buy meat without having to consider at all that someone had to kill and dress the animal. Before refrigeration, you went to get your meat fresh from a butcher. A butcher deals with meat cutting from the carcasses of dead animals, something many people were happy to have someone else do.

The job brought about some interesting "actually innocent but sounds scary" jokes:

> *It was a busy day in the butcher-shop. The butcher yelled to the boy who helped him out in the shop: "Hurry up, John, remember to cut off Mrs. Murphy's leg, break Mrs. Jones's bones, and don't forget to slice Mrs. Johnson's tongue."*

This follows the same lines:

> *Mrs. Smith had given the butcher her daily order over the telephone. Later in the day, she decided to change the order she had given for some liver.*
>
> *Calling up the butcher, she said "You remember that I gave you an order this morning for a pound of liver?"*
>
> *"Yes," answered the butcher.*
>
> *"Well, I find that I can get along without it, and you need not send it."*
>
> *Before she could put down the receiver, she heard the butcher say to someone in the store, "Cut out Mrs. Smith's liver. She says she can get along without it."*

Back before ice packs, people would put a slice of raw meat on cuts and bruises. The rationale was that the meat felt cool and could reduce swelling, and it was thought to remove the impurities from the wound. In modern times we know it may feel cool, but it's just not very sanitary.

> *"Look here," said the young man walking into the butcher's shop with two black eyes, "could you sell me beef for both my eyes without asking about how I got them?"*
>
> *"I'll do my best, sir," the butcher replied, then cut the meat and wrapped it for the youth. When he received payment, he pushed the money back to the youth and said, "Tell you what— I'll give it to you free if you tell me the story."*

The joke being it must be some exciting story, and the butcher wants to hear it.

Censorship

Censors for television, radio, websites, etc. go through various media taking out things which some viewers may find offensive before it is published or aired— often profanity and nudity.

This still occurs for media trying to get mass appeal and are concerned with ratings, but it's a little dated, as the Internet permits people and small broadcasters much more freedom of expression, with less restrictions.

Here's an old poem about how censors like seeing the things they are cutting out just as much as the people who want to see it.

A practical censor,
When examining smut,
Gets a good look
Before saying "tut-tut."

This one is a joke about how some books being published in the 1960s were naughtier than some people liked:

Have you read some of the books they're selling these days? One was so daring; the last page was a summons!

Meaning a summons to court for reading the book.

"TV Guide" was a weekly listing of all the shows on all the channels— it's still around, just online and very limited physical form:

This TV season the accent is on total frankness in language, approach, and subject matter. I know because my TV Guide came in a plain brown wrapper.

When pornographic magazines were delivered, they promised to be delivered in a "plain brown wrapper" so as not to embarrass you in front of your mailman, family, or neighbors.

Checkbooks

Before electronic pay methods to move money and keep track of spending, people would fill out and use paper checks and keep track of their spending in a checkbook.

> *Father's Day was its usual vast success.*
> *Many dads received appropriate gifts of*
> *clean, new checkbooks.*

The humor here is that the children are giving their father something to help him give money to his children.

> *Landlady: That new boarder must either be*
> *a married man or a widower.*
> *Daughter: He told me he's a bachelor,*
> *though.*
> *Landlady: I don't believe that, because each*
> *time he opens up his checkbook he*
> *turns his back to me.*

A person who could read quickly and upside down could glance over the person's spending history and current balance if their checkbook was opened a certain way. She's assuming he turns away because he had experience keeping his spending secret from a wife.

Classical Elements

The Greek philosopher Empedocles was the first to group classical elements into earth, air, fire, and water around 450 BC. The following references that.

> *A gentleman talking of the four elements expressed great admiration at the creation of water.*
>
> *"There's nothing very special about that," said a listener. "Even I can make water!"*

"Making water" is a polite term for urination.

Coca-Cola

This deals with the two major soft drink manufacturers, Coke and Pepsi, and "Things go better with Coke" was an advertising jingle for Coca-Cola in the 1960s.

> *A planeload of Pepsi was flying over the deepest, darkest jungle. The engine developed trouble, and the plane went down. The Pepsi company sent out a rescue team to find the Pepsi and the crew. The rescuers found the wreckage, but there was no sign of the Pepsi or the crew. Finally, they came upon a cannibal village. They asked the chief if he had seen the crew and the Pepsi.*

The chief said, "Yes, we ate the crew and drank the Pepsi."

The rescuer said, "My gosh, you ate their arms?"

"Yes, we ate the arms and washed them down with Pepsi."

"You ate their legs?"

"Yes, we ate their legs and washed them down with the Pepsi."

The rescuer then said: "I hate to ask you, but did you eat their... you know... 'things'?"

Chief said: "Oh, no. Things go better with Coke."

The word "things" here meaning penises.

Condoms

In many places these days you can buy condoms for birth control right off the shelf, but in the mid-20th century, they were kept behind the counter, partly to deter theft and partly because they weren't considered appropriate to have out in the open where women and children could see them. People were then embarrassed to ask the pharmacist for them. This joke plays on that:

A man goes in for a job interview, and he's constantly winking one eye. The interviewer is patient with this and finds the man is an excellent candidate for the job but must ask about the winking.

"You're a perfect fit for us," he says, "however I hope you don't mind me asking, but I noticed you're constantly winking your eye. I don't want our customers to get the wrong idea about you."

"Oh, that's a rare condition I have, I can get you a doctor's note about it. All I have to do is take some aspirin and it's gone."

The man starts pulling boxes of condoms out of his pockets and piles them on the desk in front of him before finding an aspirin. He takes one, and the winking stops.

"I'm glad to see that," the interviewer says looking at the pile of boxes on his desk. "What's with all the condoms?"

The man sighs. "Have you ever gone into a drugstore, winking nonstop and said, 'You got any aspirin?'"

The drugstore workers always assumed the man was implying he wanted condoms, not aspirin.

Condoms made from sheep bladders (yes, this was before disposable latex "rubbers") could be washed and reused.

A man entered a drug store and went to the back counter. "Do you have any condoms?" he asked the clerk.

"What kind, the 25-cent ones or the 50-cent kind?" asked the clerk.

"Well, what's the difference?" asked the man.

"The 50-cent ones you can wash, and use again and again," he was informed. "Fine," he said, "that's a good deal, I'll take one."

In a few weeks he returned to the drug store, went up to the clerk and said: "I want to buy more condoms, but not the ones that can be washed."

"Why not, what's the matter?" the clerk asked. "Didn't it work all right?"

"It did," retorted the man, "but I got a nasty note from my laundry lady."

Generally, you'd hand wash them yourself, not give them to another person to clean - a fact that the gentleman didn't consider.

This next joke doesn't involve condoms but still expresses the discomfort of going into a drugstore to ask for something sexually related. The man is horny and is going into the store for bromide - there was a myth that bromide damped male sexual arousal.

A man is walking down the street and finds he is horny - with an erection to match, so he walked into a nearby pharmacy to get some bromide. He was somewhat embarrassed when he found a woman behind the counter. "Pardon me," he said, "but I'd like to see the boss."

"I'm the boss," said the woman.

"Well can I talk to a... male... clerk?" he said.

"We haven't any," the owner replied, "My sister and I are co-owners here. You can tell me what you want, though. I won't be embarrassed."

"Well," said the stranger, "I've got an awful boner. What can you give me for it?"

"Just a minute," said the woman, and went to the back of the drug store. In a few minutes she returned. "I've just been talking it over with my sister, and the best we can give you is a hundred dollars each."

They're willing to pay him for sex as if he was a prostitute.

Some versions of this joke included offering the entire store in exchange, but that's pushing it even in a joke - or I'm missing a punchline.

Drugstores

A "drugstore" originally meant "drugs," as in medications. In the early 20th century, pharmacies branched out into other sales to be more profitable, in the process of becoming more like a general store or a lunch counter. This led to jokes about "pharmacists" who were doing anything except being a pharmacist.

Customer: I want a bottle of aspirin, please.
Pharmacist: I'm sorry sir, this is a drug store. Can I interest you in an alarm clock, some nice leather goods, a few radio parts, or a toasted cheese sandwich?

And…

First Pharmacist: I understand Jones has been given a medal by the Society for Pharmaceutical Research.
Second Pharmacist: Yes, he has invented three new sandwiches.

And…

Customer: Good heavens, I'm poisoned! It must have been the sandwiches my wife gave me!
Pharmacist: Absolutely. I'm telling you you're taking a chance each time you eat a sandwich that isn't prepared by a registered pharmacist.

And…

First Person: Why do you keep your postage stamps in the medicine cabinet?

Second Person: Why not? I buy them at the drug store!

This next one refers to Mustard Plaster, which is a mustard-based home remedy spread on aches and pains, not the condiment, as this pharmacist assumes out of sandwich-making habit.

Customer: Mustard Plaster, please.
Pharmacist: We're out of mustard. How about mayonnaise?

A "truss" was a leather and steel medical appliance that you wore if you had a hernia. It had to be fitted on you by a pharmacist, who measured your waist and crotch to get the fit just right. The pharmacist is confused why a child would be asking about this device children don't generally need.

A ten-year-old boy walks into a pharmacy and goes to the candy counter in the back of the store, behind which the pharmacist is working. "Do you fit trusses here?" asks the boy.

"Why, yes," replies the pharmacist, looking puzzled.

"Well, wash your hands and give me five cents' worth of jellybeans."

The boy doesn't want hands that touched private parts touching his jelly beans without being washed first. A modern version of this joke has a woman standing next to a sign that says, “Hand jobs $10, cheese sandwiches $5.” A man walks up and says, “Wash your hands and give me a cheese sandwich.”

This one’s misunderstanding is a little dated in the age of email and uses the double meaning of a tablet for a pill, or a tablet for pad of paper. In this joke as opposed to the above, the pharmacist is actually trying to be a pharmacist:

Customer: I want a tablet.
Pharmacist: What kind of tablet?
Customer: A yellow one.
Pharmacist: No, what’s wrong with you?
Customer: I want to write a letter.

And…

Pharmacist: Did the mustard plaster do you any good?
Customer: Yes; but it does bite the tongue!

They were eating it instead of putting it on their skin.

Duels

Since antiquity and finally becoming illegal in most places by the 20th century, a duel to the death was one of the ways one could defend your honor against a real or perceived insult. Here’s a play on names involving a duel; it’s a shortened form of several different poems and tongue twisters further confusing things but are essentially the same joke.

Mr. Knott and Mr. Shott were in a duel. In the end, Knott was shot and Shott was not.

The following joke includes a Frenchman and an Englishman, but you can switch them and use any nationality or characters you choose.

A Frenchman and an Englishman had a duel in a dark room. The Frenchman, not wanting to take a life, fired his gun up the chimney and killed the Englishman. [1]

The Frenchman above was trying to be kind and satisfy honor by discharging his weapon up the chimney without killing the Englishman. Unfortunately, the Englishman, not wanting to be in the duel, was trying to escape up the chimney.

Esso Gasoline

Esso is a brand of ExxonMobil. In the 1960s they had an advertising campaign "Put a Tiger in your Tank." They even gave out promotional tiger tails you could hang off your gas cap, so it looked like you actually had "a tiger in your tank."

---

[1] This joke, as I found it, had the Englishman as the one firing up the chimney, but I switched it around to put the Frenchman as the honorable one here to have a little balance with all the "French Surrender" jokes from World War II in this book.

Q: Did you know that before Esso decided on the "Put a Tiger in Your Tank" campaign, they thought about having an insect as a mascot?
A: It turned out no one wanted to be an "Esso Bee."

"Esso Bee" rhymes with "S.O.B." which is a mild curse meaning "Son of [a] bitch."

Fairy Liquid

In the 1980s, the British dishwashing soap Fairy Liquid's jingle was: "Now hands that do dishes can feel soft as your face, with mild green Fairy Liquid."

A man walks into a seafood restaurant. He goes over to the tank to pick what to eat and asks to have a small light green squid with a tiny moustache. The waiter calls for the cook, Gervais, to grab the squid, kill it, and cook it. Gervais takes the squid into the kitchen, grabs a big cleaver, and is about to kill the poor creature when he sees that its eyes are filled with tears of fear.

Pitying the poor animal, he goes back to the waiter and says he can't do it. The waiter nods and tells Hans the dishwasher to do it instead. So, Hans takes the poor squid, grabs the cleaver, and is about to bring it down, when he too looks at the squid's sad, frightened eyes, and he, too, cannot bring himself to kill the squid.

Defeated, the waiter goes back to the customer and says, "Well, it just goes to show... Hans that does dishes can be as soft as Gervais, with mild green hairy lip squid!"

Flesh Color

Most cultures ended up with a distinct average skin color among themselves for a lot of history, with a little mixing here and there. Before communication and travel came about, calling a specific color that matched everyone's skin "flesh" wasn't really a problem.

As people moved around and populations changed, Crayola Crayons were one specific item that was pointed out as an example of this being outdated— in 1903 when they were first sold, the color we now know from the crayons as "peach" was labeled "flesh" or "flesh tint" because it matched most Caucasian's skin color. It stayed that way until the 1960s. Of course, we know flesh comes in a wide range of hues, and any connection to skin tone has been dropped from crayon names to let the person who is doing the coloring choose for themselves.

The debate is brought up in this joke regarding women's stockings.

Customer: Do you carry flesh-colored stockings?
Salesperson: Yes, do you want pink, yellow, or black?

Pink refers to "White skin," yellow refers to "oriental skin" and black refers to "black skin."

Five and Ten Stores

Today in the United States, "dollar stores" are the standard "cheap" store, even though many things in them cost more than a dollar now. Back in the early to mid-20th century, they were called "five and ten" stores or versions of that, such as "five and dime". The name implied everything cost a nickel (5 cents) or a dime (10 cents).

First Person: I bought it at the fifteen-cent store.
Second Person: You mean the five and ten?
First Person: Well, 5 and 10 are 15.

General Electric Lightbulbs

General Electric or "G.E." was famous for manufacturing light bulbs for over a hundred years, but they have branched out into other products. Folks these days generally don't have a "preferred light bulb brand" or even know what brands of light bulbs are out there.

First Person: Spell "image" and then say "lightbulb."
Second Person: I-M-A-G-E lightbulb.

Said out loud, the punchline sounds like "I am a G.E. lightbulb."

Gleem Toothpaste

Gleem was a popular brand of toothpaste in the 1950s and 1960s, being discontinued in 2014.

My grandfather still has a gleam in his eye; he keeps missing his mouth with his toothbrush.

"Gleam" (a twinkle of light), rhymes with Gleem.

When I first read this joke, I thought to myself "Maybe the grandfather should use Aim." (Aim being another brand of toothpaste.)

Ice

Before refrigeration, ice was cut in blocks from frozen freshwater lakes, towed to towns, and kept in icehouses covered in sawdust or straw for insulation. Ice could be kept all summer this way.

Diner: I say! This water's full of crumbs!
Waiter.: That's not crumbs! That's only the sawdust off the ice!

As if it made a big difference what the things floating around in your water were.

First Person: What's the matter? You look chilled.
Second Person: Right you are, the fact is, I attended a party the other evening and everything they served was iced.

"Chilled" means to look a little cold or apprehensive, like "chilled to the bone." He's joking that it's because of the social having iced food, which was a novelty.

Ivory Soap

Ivory bar soap, first sold in the 1870s, is unusual in that it floats, which was helpful for finding it in a bathtub, showers did not become commonplace in private homes until the late 20th century. The advertising slogan "It Floats" first appeared in 1891. There is an urban legend the company didn't mind spreading that a worker had left the soap mix running too long, putting extra air into the soap so the discovery was an accident, but in 2004 documentation was found that a company chemist had figured it out during their own research for that purpose.

A man and his wife were on an ocean voyage when the wife unexpectedly passed away. They held a burial at sea.

The next night the husband kept hearing a ghostly voice whispering "It floats... it floats..." and the man just froze in bed, listening in fear.

The next night, the same. "It floats... it floats..."

On the third night again came the voice, "It floats... it floats..."

He whispered in terror "What floats?"

The voice said, "Ivory, the soap that floats!"

The joke being the building up of tension and releasing that tension with the commercial jingle.

Ketchup

Ketchup today is usually associated with tomato ketchup but was originally a term for any similar sauce. There are many tomato ketchup jokes like the one below. What makes this outdated was using mushrooms. Mushroom ketchup still exists, but it not what most people think of when they hear the word "ketchup."

If you are on a train, and it's running late, throw some mushrooms on the track and it will ketchup.

The mushrooms would be crushed into a sauce by the train, and "ketchup" and "catch up" are puns.

Lynching in the United States

Lynching is to execute a person, often by hanging, without giving them their due process in court. Hanging wasn't the only way the execution was done, but lynching was the blanket term for many ways of execution. After the Civil War, lynchings were used as a way of trying to uphold white supremacy in the American South. Sometimes the lynched were actually guilty, but sometimes not.

This was perceived to be a part of American culture outside of America. Postcards with photographs of lynchings were sold, further advertising that part of America.

Eugene Field (1850-1895), listed here, was an American humorist known for essays and children's poetry.

> *Eugene Field was at a recent dinner in London when the conversation turned to the subject of lynching in the United States. It was the general opinion that a large percentage of Americans met death at the end of a rope. Finally, the hostess turned to Field, who had taken no part in the conversation, and said:*
>
> *"You, sir, must have often seen these affairs."*
>
> *"Yes," he replied, "we take a kind of hometown pride in seeing which city can show the greatest number of lynchings yearly."*

"Oh, do tell us about a lynching you have seen yourself," broke in half a dozen voices at once.

"The night before I sailed for England," he said, "I was giving a dinner at a hotel to a party of intimate friends when a waiter spilled a plate of soup over the gown of a lady at an adjoining table. The gown was utterly ruined, and the gentlemen of her party at once seized the waiter, tied a rope around his neck, and at a signal from the injured lady swung him into the air."

"Horrible," said the hostess with a shudder. "And did you actually see this yourself?"

"Well, no," admitted the American apologetically. "Just at that moment I happened to be downstairs killing the chef for putting mustard in the blanc mange."

Blanc mange is a dessert.

Field is having a bit of fun exaggerating the amount of lynching and killing going on in America. It did happen, but not to the levels implied in the joke.

Military 24-Hour Clock

The 24-hour clock divides the day into 24 separate hours instead of looping 12:00 a.m. and p.m. This is sometimes called "military time," but is used in many industries (and a few countries) to prevent confusing an a.m. time with a p.m. time. All you have to do to convert from a 24-hour clock time to 12-hour clock time is to subtract 12 from all times including and after "13:00" (1:00 p.m.) and add 12 to p.m. times to convert the other way.

The following can have the General here be any person who works in an industry that uses the 24-hour clock, such as aviation, military, etc.

> *A doctor was giving a General a physical. Taking his history, he asked "When was the last time you had sex?"*
>
> *The General answered, "Nineteen fifty-five."*
>
> *The Doctor said, "That long ago?*
>
> *Looking at his watch, the General said, "It wasn't that long ago, it's only twenty-one-oh-five now."*

The joke is that the doctor assumes that the General last had sex in the year 1955, but the General meant a little over an hour previously, at 19:55 (7:55 p.m.). The side issue that the doctor probably should have asked "are you sexually active" instead of "when did you last have sex," or why on earth the General is having a doctor's appointment at 9:00 p.m. are side points required for the joke to work as written.

It's a dated joke because 1955 is a long time ago. A person doing some quick math in the year 2025 would say, "Why would the doctor simply think that last having sex 70 years ago was normal? This General must be over 90 years old! Why isn't he retired?" Since you're reading this book in the future, I'm sure that time jump has gotten worse.

You *can* update this for right now, but the teller has to do some math first – and doesn't everyone love doing mathematics on the fly for a laugh? Make the sex happen late in the evening. Most years in the 21st century would be around 8:00 p.m. such as 2015 (8:15 p.m.), and have the appointment happen in the morning "It's oh-nine-hundred (09:00 a.m.) now."

However... future readers will have to exclude 40 years (2060-2099) from the possible "sex time" because there's only 60 minutes in an hour, but 100 years in a century - 2065 would be 8:65 p.m., which doesn't make sense. It was the same issue with 1960-1999, which is probably why I didn't find an updated version of this joke anywhere.

Adding to that confusion, we don't pronounce the years from 2000-2009 (8:00 p.m. - 8:10 p.m.) "twenty hundred to twenty-oh-nine" as military time does; we call them "two thousand to two thousand nine." The joke continues to complicate itself.

Alas, this one will become un-updateable after the mid 2400s (12:00 a.m. to 12:59 a.m.). We'll let those future comedians have a final moment of silence for it.

Milk

Milk spoils quickly. Until the 1960s when supermarkets and home refrigeration made it easy to buy and keep milk in the home, a milkman would deliver it to your home.

This joke involves the disconnect of city living from country living, that the people who deliver the milk for a living would have never seen a cow in real life.

A man living in the heart of London has recently bought a cow, which he keeps in his backyard. Thirty milkmen have already been seen peeking over the wall to see what a cow looks like.

When you let fresh straight-out-of-the-cow milk sit, it separates into high-fat cream on the top and watery low-fat milk on the bottom. The process of homogenizing milk (which keeps those layers mixed even if it sits for a while) was invented in 1892 in France. It slowly became more popular until the 1950s when it became essentially the only way milk was sold.

This is a "women lie about their age" joke; it's the act being portrayed that dates the joke.

My wife says she's under 30 years old, but she shakes the milk before pouring it.

The wife is used to unhomogenized milk, implying that as of the timeframe of the joke she's a little old-fashioned.

Paris Green

Paris green is a pigment first manufactured in 1814, which had a large amount of arsenic in it. In the 1860s it was recognized as a good insecticide, too. The color tends to degrade quickly in paintings and it's highly toxic to humans, so it isn't used anymore. Crab lice are often sexually transmitted and are still with us today. The joke here is that more than simply the lice were eradicated.

Two young movie actresses from Hollywood met in the studio during the lunch rest period, and one complained to the other that she had been troubled for quite a time with crab lice. "How can I get rid of them?" she asked.

"Just rub in some Paris green," said her friend, "that'll kill 'em."

A week or so later they met again, and the first girl asked: "Did you rub in that Paris green as I told you?"

"Yes," she replied.

"Did it kill the crabs?"

"Yep, and a couple of directors too."

Pawnshops

Pawnbrokers "Pawnshops" still exist, that will buy items off of you for resale. It used to be nearly every pawn shop had three balls on its sign or displayed. The original meaning of the three balls is uncertain, but it used to be a sign of a pawnshop that even the illiterate could identify.

Q: What is the meaning of the three balls in front of a pawn brokers?
A: Two to one that you won't get money for it.

The joke is that the odds things are accepted for money are "Two to one against" or "2:1 against," meaning you've got a one third chance of getting money for what you want to sell there.

Pornography

What is porn, exactly? No one can agree on that. What is certain is that there is a lot of disagreement with the definition. The internet has made it very easy to find, and folks still aren't agreed on how good or bad this is. I really doubt they'll agree on anything anytime soon, either.

This is one about someone asking for erotic literature and turns into a pun.

> *Customer: Do you have any pornographic literature?*
> *Clerk: Gosh, we don't even have a pornograph.*

It's a bit of nonsense wordplay with "pornography" and "phonograph" (record player).

Magazines were the most popular way to get porn for many years, bought at an adult bookstore, or from the top rack (or under the counter) at a newsstand, or delivered to your home in a wrapper so everyone didn't see what it was.

> *"Is it bad when you refer to all porno magazines as 'dates'?"* [1]

There were many porn magazines, but *Playboy* was the "respectable" one because it had lots of non-nudity content:

---

[1] Patton Oswalt

interviews, cartoons, editorials, a joke page. A common quip was:

I only read Playboy magazine for the articles.

The centerfold was a large fold-out photo of the "Playmate of the Month."

Q: Did you hear about the new version of
Playboy for married men?
A: It has the same centerfold every month.

A joke on how your wife is the same every month.

This next starts out as seeming to be a compliment to a woman until it likens her to a stack of magazines, "issues" being "mental problems."

Damn girl, are you Playboy magazine?
Because you are a pile of issues.

You kept your pornographic collection hidden from your children— even your spouse, if they didn't like that sort of thing. Many children of the 20th century remember discovering their parents' collections.

I have discovered there is something worse than finding your grandpa's stash of Playboys... It's figuring out the reason why some of the pages are stuck together!

It's dried semen. A modern version would be "why is your phone sticky?"

The following is a dark humor joke:

> *Q: What's more horrifying than finding a stack of your father's Playboys in the basement?*
> *A: Realizing one of them is still breathing.*

Playboy, before it was used as a magazine title, it meant a young man with a lot of wealth and time for pleasure and in this joke, they are dead in a basement. The father is assumed to be a serial killer.

National Geographic was a popular travel and information magazine.

> *First Man: My wife lets me subscribe to National Geographic and Playboy for the same reason.*
> *Second Man: What's that?*
> *First Man: Because with both magazines, I get to see places I'll never get to visit.*

National Geographic was not a pornographic magazine, but they sold more copies when they included pictures of faraway tribes that didn't have civilized things like clothes. It was not in every issue, and the intention was educational, so it usually got past censorship.

Q: What's the difference between a naked white woman and a naked black woman?
A: One is on the cover of Playboy while the other is on the cover of National Geographic.

Until the advent of the video cassette recorder in the early 1980s and the internet in the 1990s, most people who wanted to see pornographic movies had to leave their house and go to a theater playing the movies.

The theaters varied. Some were reputable theaters that happened to be showing a foreign movie which had a lot of nudity or discussed sex but was still essentially a clean theater like any other. Other theaters were less reputable, where people sat to be alone to masturbate, hook up with others, or do drugs.

It was a common stereotype that celebrities and movie stars would wear trenchcoats and sunglasses when they went out so that people wouldn't recognize them in public places. This is about keeping your identity secret while going to an adult theater.

Remember when movie stars wore sunglasses so they wouldn't be recognized? Now the audience wears them!

Another term for pornographic movies was a "skin flick" because it showed "skin" and using the term "flick" for movies is a reference to the flicker of old projectors.

Remember the good old days when a skin flick was how you got rid of a bug?

Film associations eventually introduced ratings for all films so filmgoers would have some idea on what they would be seeing, and if they could take their children to a certain show. The "X" rating was originally intended to mean any film with large amounts of violence, nudity, or sexual content, but it was the sexual films that became associated with X.[1]

Every time I suggest to my wife we go see an adult movie she starts reciting the alphabet. "X? Y?"

A pun on the letter "Y" and the question "why?"

Our local movie theater coupled a Charlie Chaplin film with an X-rated movie. It gives you your choice of tramps.

Charlie Chaplain was a silent movie star, famous for his vagabond character "The Tramp" and a tramp also being a term for a loose woman.

You can tell who the good guys are in X-rated movies because they wear white socks.

---

[1] In 1990 the Motion Picture Association of America introduced the NC-17 "No children under 17" rating because the X rating, not having been copyrighted, had been used so much by the pornographic movie industry.

That is a reference to Western movies, popular in the early 20th century, where stereotypically the hero wore a white hat, the bad guy a black hat. This joke gets a little funnier when you think about how unimportant the "good guy vs bad guy" concept is in a porno movie— everyone just is, and their motives and background aren't as important as the sex.

> *I went to see an X-rated movie last night and the cashier wouldn't sell me a ticket. She said she had a headache.*

This is a play off the stereotype "My wife doesn't want to have sex tonight because she has a headache."

> *My wife and I went to an X-rated movie last night and it was fascinating.*
>
> *I came back from the restroom and asked her what I had missed.*
>
> *She pointed at the screen and said, "Two of that and one of that."*

The humor above is in treating a trip to an adult movie with your wife like a regular trip to the theater.

> *A pianist is hired to do background music to be added to a movie. When he's finished, the producer admits the music is needed for a pornographic movie due in theaters the next month.*

A month later, with his collar up and sunglasses on, the pianist goes to the theater to see his work in use. He sits next to another couple who are similarly in disguise. It turns out the movie is even raunchier than expected, with group sex, S&M, and even a dog. After a while, the pianist turns to the couple and says, "I'm only here to listen to my music."

They respond, "We're only here to see our dog."

The actual "going out to a theater" is required for this joke, as in modern times the pianist could simply be given a copy of the movie, and they could watch it privately at home — but this would take from the punchline that evidently the couple willingly allowed their dog to be in this movie.

This one also requires an adult movie theater:

A man steals a chicken and is on the run. Once he's escaped from the police, he shoves the chicken down his pants and ducks into a dark adult movie theater until the search gives up. He sits down in the back, next to two women. The chicken starts fidgeting, so he opens up his zipper to give it some air and he falls asleep, exhausted. The first woman nudges the other and whispers "Hey, this guy next to me has a cock out!"

Her friend doesn't even look over, saying "You've seen plenty of those before. It's no surprise here."

"Not this one," she responds, "it's eating my popcorn!" [1]

Prince Albert Tobacco

Prank calls were prevalent up until caller ID made it easy to see what number calling you was. Before then people had to answer the phone to see who was calling, and if someone was pranking you there was no way to find out who had called.

A stereotype prank telephone call would be to call a store that sold tobacco and ask if they offered Prince Albert brand tobacco in a specific container:

Caller: Do you have Prince Albert in a can?
Employee: Yes, we do.
Caller: Well, you better let him out!

Sati

Sati is the ancient Hindu custom of a widowed bride burning herself to death on her husband's funeral pyre. Publicly supporting the practice has been outlawed since 1987, but occasionally women still do it.

---

[1] There is a scene in the 1997 movie *Men in Black* where K (Tommy Lee Jones) memory-wipes a police officer (Will Smith) who next wakes up in a restaurant to K laughing and giving only the punchline to a version of this joke.

Q: Why do women commit Sati?
A: It's the first time they've seen their
husband that hot in years!

"Hot" here having the double meaning of "burning" and "sexy."

Seidlitz powder

Seidlitz powder was a laxative during the late 1800s to early 1900s. It was effervescent— like Alka-Seltzer, and bubbled when placed in water.

Here lies the body of Susan Lowder
Who burst while drinking Seidlitz powder.
Called from this world to her heavenly rest,
She should have waited till it effervesced.

It expanded in her stomach.

Servants

Servants are a step up from slavery, being hired help rather than property. Some people who hired servants didn't see the distinction, though— wages could be low and mistreatment happened. This issue went both ways— some servants would steal from their employer's homes and try to do as little work as possible.

Having servants had a slow decline over the years. The two World Wars of the 20th century had many male servants going to war and at the same time many female servants picked up better-paying factory jobs and other skilled work vacated by the men at war. Add to that the labor-saving technology and pre-prepared food introduced over the 20th century— it no longer required half a day of heavy labor to do the washing or the cooking.

> *While Willie and his mother were walking along the street, they passed an employment agency with this sign in the window:*
> *"Colored help supplied."*
> *"Look, ma," said Willie. "Is that where we got our green cook?"*

The word "colored" generally meant negro, but "green" is short for "greenhorn," which refers to someone new and inexperienced, or from a foreign land in a new one. The cook was a foreigner.

Of course, with how hard it was to keep good help. If you bragged about your servant being excellent at their job, you ran the risk of another family trying to hire them.

> *First maid [bragging about a party given by her mistress]: They all came in giant limousines, and had on the grandest clothes, and wore the biggest diamonds."*
> *Neighbor's maid: And what did they talk about?*
> *First maid: Us.*

The great irony here is that the rich and the powerful discussed the servants, of all things that could be discussed.

> *"A great many of the neighbors have called to see us since we moved out here," said the man of the house.*
>
> *"They didn't call to see us," replied his wife. "The report has gone out that we have a good cook, and they are trying to get acquainted with her."*

Good, reliable help was as hard to find as it is today.

> *First Person: Of course, you, too, must often change cooks?"*
>
> *Second Person: Oh, don't speak of it! We suffer from such a continual going and coming that we've decided this winter to equip our kitchen with a revolving door.*

And…

> *Husband: Did you tell the cook that the beefsteak was burned?*
>
> *Wife: Mercy, no! She would leave instantly. I told her it was just right, but that we preferred it to be a trifle underdone.*

And…

Wife: I wish I knew what to do with this skirt. It's good, but somewhat out of style.
Husband: Why don't you give it to the laundress?
Wife: Don't be funny, George. She's a good laundress, and I wouldn't want to offend her.

The woman the mistress meets here is pointing out the reality her situation.

A mistress had lost her cook and had telephoned in vain for another. Dinner guests were expected that night and she was desperate.

Finally, putting on her things, she went out, and she hadn't gone far when she met a neat-looking colored woman. She explained her dilemma and the colored woman listened in silence, then she said: "Where do you live, mistress?"

Seeing a ray of hope, the mistress gave the woman her home address, to be met with this reply:

"Well, just go there, look in the mirror, and you'll see your cook."

The colored woman was politely saying "you're going to have to do it yourself".

This maid has a daughter, and the assumption was that the maid was the treasure.

First Person: That's a shocking clumsy maid who served us. And Mrs. Wise said she had such a treasure."
Second Person: This maid is one she hired for the occasion. She has the treasure locked in her room for fear one of the guests might steal her.

The next joke involves training new servants. A calling card was a precursor to business cards. If you arrived and the person you were visiting was not there, you could present your calling card with your name and how you could be contacted.

Mrs. Smith hired a new servant and tried to teach him how to receive calling cards. She let herself out the front door, and when the new servant answered her ring, she gave him her card.

The next day two ladies came to visit Mrs. Smith. When they presented their cards, the alert servant hastily compared them with Mrs. Smith's card, and remarked as he closed the door:

"Your tickets are no good; you can't come in."

The servant assumed visitors had to have cards matching Mrs. Smith's calling card to gain entrance, just like tickets.

This next joke plays off the idea of "taking it easy" and "taking things."

New Maid: In my last place I always took things fairly easy.
Cook: Well, it's different here. They keep everything locked up.

This is about how a nursemaid might feel that they are better for the child than the actual parent:

Two nursemaids were wheeling their infant charges in the park when one asked the other, "Are you going to the dance tomorrow afternoon?"

"I am afraid not."

"What!" exclaimed the other. "And you are so fond of dancing!"

"I'd love to go," explained the conscientious maid, "but to tell you the truth, I am afraid to leave the baby with its mother."

And of course, a little flirting and sex happened.

"You're calling me a flirt?" exclaimed the maid, under notice to leave. "Well, I may be

a flirt, but I'm better-looking than you. You know how I know? Your husband told me."

"That will do," said her mistress, frigidly.

"But I'm not finished yet!" retorted the maid. "I can kiss better than you! You want to know who told me that?"

Angrily the mistress responded "If you mean to suggest that my husband—"

"No, it wasn't your husband this time," said the maid. "It was your chauffeur!"

This is a "take that" after being fired from a job.

Bridget had been discharged. Taking a five-dollar bill from her wage-roll, she threw it to the mistress's dog. Then the shocked mistress heard her exclaim: "I never forget a friend. That's for helping me with the dishes."

The dog helped by licking the dishes clean.

Slavery

Slavery has existed since pre-history. Slaves are essentially servants who are also considered property.

While sailing through a violent storm, a man's slaves started screaming in terror.

> *"Don't cry," he said. "I set you all free in my will."*

Of course, the same storm that would potentially kill the master would likely kill the slaves too. I like to consider that if the slaves weren't aware of this in his will until now, shoving him overboard during the storm and making it look like an accident might be an action considered by the slaves.

Sex with slaves happened, and here's an example where it's the woman after the male slave:

> *The lady of the house had a simpleminded slave. But when she got a look at how big his penis was, she lusted after him. She hid her face with a mask, so he wouldn't recognize her, and played around with him. He joined in and had sex with her.*
>
> *Later, cheerful as ever, he told to his master: "Sir, sir! I fucked a dancer, and your wife was inside!*

The joke is in the innocence of this slave, spilling the beans about having sex with the master's wife.

During the American Civil War era, Harriet Tubman was a famous abolitionist and former slave who went back to Maryland 13 times to eventually free a total of 70 more slaves.

> *Harriet Tubman freed 70 slaves, but that's only 42 people.*

The odd math for the punchline here is deeply rooted in early United States politics. The southern states wanted their entire population, including slaves, to count towards their elected state representatives –Those states wanted more power for less whites in comparison to the northern states. A compromise was reached in 1787 called the "Three-Fifths Compromise," where three-fifths of a state's slaves counted toward representatives, not the full population. The joke uses the terms "slaves" and then "people," and three-fifths of 70 is 42.

Here's another one using the same logic:

If five slaves had an orgy in the 1800s,
would it only be considered a three-way?

Temperance Movement

There have been anti-alcohol movements throughout history, the most successful of which was the United States movement which led to the prohibition of alcohol there in 1920, but that success was tempered by the fact that it was a colossal failure that was eventually repealed in 1934.

Here's a smart remark to a speaker extolling the virtues of temperance from alcohol:

He was genuinely enthusiastic about the virtues of temperance, but the audience began to doubt him. Toward the end of his lecture he squared his shoulders, held his head erect and said "I have lived in this town all my life. There are fifty-five bars and public houses, and I am proud to say that I have never been in one of them!"

A voice from the back hollered out "And which one is that?"

The voice is reversing the statement made, to mean that there's one he hasn't been in yet, but he's been in the other fifty-four.

Man: Water has killed more folks than liquor has!

Temperance Reformer: You're crazy. How do you think that?

Man: To begin with, there's the biblical flood!

Referring to the story of Noah in the Bible, where a flood killed all people on earth except for a handful.

Here's one about judging a situation before knowing all the facts.

A temperance reformer came upon a man lying on the ground. "And this is the work of rum, is it?"

"No, sir," the man replied from the ground and pointing. "This is the work of a banana peel."

This is playing off of the idea that banana peels are slippery, and the temperance reformer assumed he was a drunk.

Afterword

So there you go. A trip through the jokes of yesteryear. I hope you had some laughs and maybe learned something. I've really enjoyed this project, and don't plan to stop looking for outdated jokes.

If you enjoyed this book, or even if you *didn't* enjoy this book, I'd appreciate it if you left a review on Amazon, or your preferred book review site.

Do you know of any outdated jokes that didn't show up here? Send them to: Hartwix.Press@gmail.com

Thank you so much for reading!

Acknowledgements

I didn't write these dated jokes. Well… that's *mostly* true. There's one I made up back in the early 1990s when I was in high school, and it fit. It's among the phone book jokes and is about "getting bored by the W's". It's not my funniest; it's just dated now. So I personally account for… oh, about 0.1% of them.

In 2018 I picked up a copy of Robert Orben's 1979 book *2500 Jokes to Start 'Em Laughing* and in reading its huge amount of outdated humor I realized that the book you now hold in your hands could be written. As I worked, I first viewed him as a bit of a hack comedy writer in my mind until I learned he wrote many original jokes and published them in books for comedians to freely use - he had also been a speechwriter for then-Vice President Gerald Ford. He passed away in 2023 at 95 years old. A posthumous "thank you" for the extra inspiration and consider this an apology.

Where a joke book gave me a line from a comedian and cited the comedian (such as Judy Brown's books of comedy quotes), I put a footnote on the page giving credit and tried not to do any editing of the quote when copying from that book. I think I might have missed a few references, so if you are a comedian and see I used your line without referencing you personally, I apologize. I understand that credit gets weird there, as comedians employ writers who also deserve credit.

I did not learn until deep into the editing process that Judy Brown was sued by a group of comedians in 2008 for her multiple collections of quotes from comedians without seeking permission. I believe my book is fair use, as I am using the outdated humor to illustrate history, not simply publishing a collection of humor by itself.

Many of these jokes are long orphaned from their original source. The sources I went through culled their content from magazines like *Punch* or *Judge,* from earlier humor books, newspapers, and magazines — and even those were probably from previous sources. Take a moment of appreciation for the great unknowns who came up with a good nugget of humor, and for those other unknowns who improved upon them over the years.

As for the physical books I went through, I cannot express enough appreciation for free public libraries. Avalon Public Library and the Carnegie Public Library Main Branch in Pittsburgh, all connected through the larger Allegheny County Public Library Association— everyone I dealt with was courteous, fast, knowledgeable, and helpful.

The internet has been a great resource for finding jokes, even if finding what I was looking for was hard with all the repeats. This included sites like, but not limited to, Upjoke, Reddit, Quora, other joke sites, and several various enthusiast forums/pages with a "jokes" section.

During a web search for humor from 1910, I stumbled upon the Jack Horntip Collection https://www.horntip.com, which has been an excellent resource for old Toastmaster's books and joke books.

Project Gutenberg https://www.gutenberg.org, was also incredibly helpful. Keep keeping the past alive, folks!

Jonathan Woodworth from ArrestorWorks quickly responded to an admittedly random email asking what the heck a "television arrestor" could be. Thank you!

To all of you hundreds of people who posted a truly original dated joke online, I thank you deeply. I wish I could cite each of you here by name, but that would just be a long list of non sequitur online handles like "Basement-dweller6969" or "Mike Ock" or "IPwndUInFortnite."

And to all of you out there swapping jokes and memes online or in person, coming up with snappy quips and responses to things, who recognize that finding humor in something is often the only way to survive another day in this sometimes insane, unforgiving world...

You are my people.

Thanks

I'm lazy. I was the bright kid in school who never did his homework, yet still managed to move on to the next year and then eventually graduate with the lowest grades I could possibly get away with. The highest college degree I hold is a two-year degree in psychology. It's really hard to concentrate on "busy work" in a world with great friends, games, movies, libraries, so many things to learn and do.

As a result, you can imagine my confusion and disbelief as I sit here staring at a finished book on my laptop screen, ready for publishing.

What the hell happened to my laziness? It's never failed me before!

Before I go about patting myself on the back for finally getting something done for once, I have to stop and thank the supporting cast in this project.

To my editor, Amy Frushour Kelly, who is also my sister. She pulled no punches in treating me like a client, and not her little brother. I'm used to taking punches from my sister - but it was new territory having those punches come not as fists but as solid, logical, grammatical points and suggestions on book structure. Any mistakes the reader may still find here are all my own, not hers. Thank you, Amy. You are awesome, never let anyone ever tell you different.

To my parents and stepparents for their continued love and support. Thank you for teaching me to always read, research, and double-check information. Thank you for not holding back on jokes in front of me and doing your best to steer me right. I appreciate it every day.

To my board gaming buddy, movie-watching companion, best friend, wife, and muse: Renee'. Thank you for your love and support in this project. Words cannot express my appreciation for you in my life.

Bibliography

Hierocles and Philagrius, *Philogelos*, Translated by Annie McCabe in 2018, circa 300 AD-700 AD

Various Authors, *The Book of Anecdotes and Budget of Fun*, Geo. G. Evans, 1860

Hammerton, J.A., *Mr. Punch Awheel: The Humours of Motoring and Cycling*, Carmelite House, 1898

May, Phil, *Mr. Punch's Railway Book*, Carmelite House, 1898

Landon, Melville D., *Wit and Humor of the Age*, A.S. Gray & Company, 1890

Various Authors, *Witty Pieces for Witty Peop*le, Royal Publishing Company, 1894

Kemble, John R., *Four Hundred Laughs*, New Amsterdam Book Company, 1901

Mason, Thomas L., *Little Masterpieces of American Wit and Humor*, Volume II, Doubleday, Page and Company, 1903

No author listed. *Toasts and Maxims*, R.F. Fenno & Company, 1908

Patten, William, *Among the Humorists and After Dinner Speakers*, P. F. Collier and Son, 1909

Various Authors, *Up-to-date Smart Set Jokes #48*. I. & M. Ottenheimer Publishers (Undated, late 1910s)

Anonymous, *Jokes for all Occasions*, Edward J. Clode, 1921,1922

Mosher, Marion Dix, *More Toasts: Jokes, Stories, and Quotations*, 1922

Passeman, William, *Anecdota Americana*, Humphery Adams, 1927

Passeman, William, *Anecdota Americana: An Anthology of Tales in the Vernacular Edited without Expurgation,* Humphery Adams, 1934

Edmund, Peggy, *Toaster's Handbook*, H. W. Wilson Company, 1938

Copeland, Lewis, *10,000 Jokes, Toasts and Stories*, Garden City books, 1940, 1965

Prochnow, Herbert V., *The Toastmaster's Handbook,* Prentice Hall, Inc, 1949

Godfrey, Arthur, *Stories I Like to Tell*, Simon and Schuster, 1952

Prochnow, Herbert V., *New Guide for Toastmasters and Speakers*, Prentice Hall, Inc, 1956

Lambert, W.G., *Babylonian Wisdom Literature*, Oxford, Clarendon Press, 1960

Benardete, Doris, *Civil War Humor*, Peter Pauper Press 1963

Orben, Robert, *Joke Teller's Handbook*, Bell Publishing Company, 1966

Prochnow, Herbert V., *1,000 Quips, Stories and Illustrations for all Occasions*, Prentice Hall, Inc, 1973

Orben, Robert, *2500 Jokes to Start 'Em Laughing,* Wilshire Book Company, 1979

Meiers, Mildred, *5600 Jokes for All Occasions*, Wings Books, 1980

Berle, Milton, *Milton Berle's Private Joke File*, Three Rivers Press, 1989

Berle, Milton, *More of the Best from Milton Berle's Private Joke File*, Castle Books, 1996

Cohl, H. Aaron, *The Friars Club Encyclopedia of Jokes*, Black Dog & Leventhal, 1997

Kostick, Anna et al, *Good Clean Jokes: 3650 Jokes, Puns and Riddles*, Tess Press, 1998

Brown, Judy, *Joke Soup: 1,217 of the Funniest Jokes from the Best Comedians*, Andrews McMeel Publishing, 1998

Brown, Judy, *Joke Stew: 1,349 More Hilarious Servings from Today's Hottest Comedians*, Andrews McMeel Publishing, 2000

No Author Listed, *1001 Cool Jokes*, Hinkler Books, 2000

Dahl, Michael, *Everything Kids' Joke Book*, Simon and Schuster, 2001

Simon, Francesca, *Horrid Henry's Joke Book*, Sourcebooks Jabberwocky, 2004

Brown, Judy, *Squeaky Clean Comedy*, Andrews McMeel Publishing, 2005

Goldstein, Jack, *101 Amazing Jokes*, Andrews UK, 2013

Index

2

24-hour clock, 312–14

9

9/11. See September 11th 2001 Attacks

A

Aberystwyth,Wales, 87
Achille Lauro Hijacking, The, 272
Adams Express Shipping Company, 285
Africa, 241
Agent Orange, 259
AIDS Epidemic, 269–71
Airplanes, 57, 197–205
- Air insurance, 203
- Air pressure, 202
- Alitalia (airline), 204
- Concorde, The, 204
- El Al (airline), 204
- Flight attendants, 202, 204
- Jet planes, 200
- Lufthansa (airline), 245
- Propellers, 199
- Security, 205
- United (airline), 204

Alaska, 259–60
All Shook Up (Song), 24
American Civil War, The, 23, 172, 210–11, 332
An Essay on Criticism, 175
Antennas, 101–2
Arkansas (US State), 46
Army, 43
Atwood, Harry N., 198
Automobiles, 11, 175–92
- Engine choke, 187
- Hand crank starter, 184
- Hand signals, 186, 204
- Odometers, 188, 189
- Speedometer, 183
- Turn Signal, 194
- Turn signals, 185

B

Barbershops, 285–87
Beater (hunting job), 288
Beatles, The, 265
Bell, Alexander Graham, 66
Bellows, 111
Berman, Shelly, 205
Bicycles, 174–75
Big Mac, 288–89
Blonde joke, 22
Boats. See Ships
Boone, Daniel, 253
Branch Davidian, 192, 280
Brandt, Alicia, 93
Budweiser, 273
Burma-Shave, 289–91
Bush, George H. W., 276
Butcher Shops, 181, 291–93
Buttons, Red, 203

C

Cable TV, 99
Cabs, 192–97
Cameras. See
Carpenter, Karen, 267
Carpet Beater, 111–12
Cart. See Wagons

Cass Elliot, 267
Censorship, 293–94
Chad (early meme), 243
Chaise. See Wagons
Challenger, Space Shuttle, 272–74
Chaplin, Charlie, 321
Chappaquiddick Incident, 262–64
Charles III, King, 271
Charles, Prince, 271
Checkbooks, 294–95
Chewing tobacco. See Spittoons
Chicago, Illinois, 61, 104, 212
Chicken stealing, 31, 40, 323
Cinema. See Movies
Clapton, Eric, 278–79
Classical Elements, 295–96
Clocks and Timepieces, 46, 116–20
Coal Shortage, 222–23
Coca-Cola, 296–97
Cold War, The, 246–48
Colonel Bogey March, The (song), 235
Columbia, Space Shuttle. See Challenger, Space Shuttle
Computers, 141–45
Condoms, 297–300
Culture Club, 222

D

Daguerreotype. See Photography
Dangerfield, Rodney, 204
Dardanelles (waterway), 221
Def Lepard, 272
Dewey, Thomas, 248
Diana, Princess, 271
Dictaphone, 137
Disneyworld Paris, 246
Drive-in Theater, 64–66, 203
Drugstores, 300–303
Duck Soup (movie), 130
Duels, 303–4
Dumb person (placeholder) jokes, 21, 33, 36, 48, 66, 70, 96, 104, 106, 138, 140, 144, 165, 171, 188

E

Earliest Known Joke, 16
Early internet, 105–7
Edison. See Phonograph
Edison, Thomas Alva, 127
Edward VIII, King, 233
Elevators, 160–62
Empedocles (Greek philosopher), 296
Empire State Building, 230
Encyclopedias, 47–49
Encyclopedia Brittanica, 48, 49
Nelson's Encyclopaedia, 49
Esso Gasoline, 304–5
Eye dialect, 31, 173

F

Fairy (Dishwashing Liquid), 305–6
Farrar Browne, Charles. See Ward, Artemis
Farting, 32
Fax Machines, 103–5
Feghoot, 29
Hans that does dishes can be as soft as Gervais, 306

It's a long way to tip a rarey, 219
Super Callused Fagile Mystic, 261
Things go better with Coke, 297
Two obese Pattys, special Ross, 289
Field, Eugene, 311
Fields, W.C., 223
Five and Ten Stores, 307
Flander's Fields, 221
Flatiron, 114–15
Flesh color, 306–7
Flick. See Movies
Fokker, Anthony, 245
Ford Pinto, 264
Foster, Glen, 69
Fountain Pens, 120–22

G

Gallagher, 98
Gallup polls, 249
Gandhi, Mahatma, 260–61
Garfield, James A., 185
Gas Meter, 126–27
Gas Stove, 114
Geico insurance, 54
Gender switch, 75, 299
General Electric Lightbulbs, 307–8
German measles, 247
Germany, 234, 236, 237, 238, 240, 241, 245, 247, 290
Gleem Toothpaste, 308
Going Postal. See Post Office Shootings
Gold Rush, 210
Gramaphone. See Phonograph
Great Depression, The, 230–31
Greek, 16
Guiding Light, The, 64

H

Hall-Mills Murder Case, The, 227–28
Hansom, Joseph, 192
Hazelwood, Joseph, 275
Heating, 115–16
Heaven's Gate (cult), 268
Hitchhiker's Guide to the Galaxy, The, 70
Honolulu, Hawaii, 248
Hopalong Cassidy, 215
Horsefly, 176
Horses, 147–56, 171, 176, 177, 180, 182
Hudson, Rock, 270

I

I Want to Be an Angel (song), 183
Ice, 308–9
In Flanders Fields (poem), 222
Indian (from India), 54
Indian (North America). See Native American
Indiana (US State), 271
Inter-Continental Ballistic Missiles, 248
Internet. See Early internet
Irish, 32, 50, 218
Irish Famine (1845-1852), 207
Irish Washerwoman, The (song), 263
It's a Long Way to Tipperary (song), 218–19

Italy, 204, 241, 290
Ivory Soap, 10, 309–10

J

Japan, 87, 89, 241, 290
Kariuizawa, 89
Johnstown Flood, The, 211–13
Johnstown, Pennsylvania, 212
Jonestown Massacre, The, 267–68

K

Kennedy Cavendish, Kathleen, 261
Kennedy Jr, Joseph P, 263
Kennedy Sr, Joseph P., 263
Kennedy, Edward "Teddy", 262–64
Kennedy, Edward M., 264
Kennedy, Joan Bennett, 264
Kennedy, John F., 23, 261, 264
Kennedy, Joseph P, 261
Kennedy, Robert F., 261, 264
Kennedy, Rose, 261, 263
Ketchup, 310
Kilroy. See Chad (early meme)
King, Rodney, 277–78
Klinghoffer, Leon, 272
Kopechne, Mary Jo, 262, 264
Korean-War, The (Lack of jokes from), 23

L

Lady Gaga, 25
Landing on the Moon, 261–62
Lennon, John, 246
Lester, Buddy, 34
Let Me Call You Sweetheart, 216–17
Lincoln, Abraham, 22, 185, 253
Linotype machine, 46
Lombard, Penelope, 60
London, England, 194, 205, 240, 245, 255, 269, 311, 315
Los Angeles Riots, 277–78
Lucky Strike (cigarettes), 246
Lynching, 310–12

M

Magazines. See Pornography
Mandel, Howie, 205
Manifest Destiny, 256
Mary Poppins, 260–61
McAuliffe, Christa, 274
McCartney, Linda, 265
McCartney, Paul, 265
Mena, Arkansas, 46
Mendoza, John, 93
Messerschmitt (Airplane manufacturer), 245
Microfilm, 102–3
Military Time, 312–14
Milk, 314–15
Milkmen, 314–15
Miller, Larry, 69
Mollie and I and the Baby (song), 128
Monica, Corbett, 203
Moon Landing, 261–62
Mothballs, 122–24
Moths, 122–24
Movies, 64–66
Pornographic, 320–24
Mustard gas, 259

N

Nabors, Jim, 270
Nation, Carrie, 215
National Geographic, 319
Native American, 54, 90, 117, 153, 256
Nesbit, Evelyn. See Thaw/White Shooting, The
New York City, 56, 61, 68, 86, 204, 222, 229, 248, 278
Newspaper
  Paperboy, 42
Newspapers, 41–47, 47, 50
  Comics page, 44
  Home uses, 45
  Paperboy, 41, 42
No Man's Land, 221
Nye, Edgar Wilson "Bill", 149

O

Orwell, George, 247
Our American Cousin, 22
Outdated topic (definition), 20
Outhouses, 109–10

P

Paris Green, 315–16
Paris, France, 236, 244, 246, 248
Parks, Tom, 92, 94
Paul Reubens, 279–80
Pawnshops, 316–17
Pee-wee Herman. See Paul Reubens
People's Temple, The, 267
Pepsi, 296–97
Philogelos, 16
  Jokes from, 16, 331, 332
Phones. See Telephone
Phonograph, 116, 127–37, 183
  Effects on Musicians, 132–33
  Skipping, 133–34
  Speeds and sides, 137
  Talking Machines, 127–31
Photography, 57–61
  Developing film, 57–60
Pittsburgh, Pennsylvania, 86
Playboy, 9, See Pornography
Poker Face (Song), 25
Pope, Alexander, 175
Pornography, 317–24
Post Office, 248
Post Office Shootings, 274–75
Postal. See Post Office Shootings
Prefabricated Houses, 126
Presley, Elvis, 24
Prince Albert Tobacco, 324
Prohibition. See United States Prohibition
Punchline (Joke part), 15

Q

Quayle, Dan, 276

R

Radio, 44, 51, 61–64, 96, 134, 168
Railroads. See Trains
Record Player. See Phonograph
Reeve, Christopher, 282
Reno Divorce, 232
Rhea, Carol, 94
Rock Music, 251–52
Rodney King Incident, The, 277–78

Rogers and Hammerstein, 249
Rogers, Will, 227

S

Sahl, Mort, 34, 255
San Francisco, California, 248
Sati, 324–25
Scottish, 50
Sears Mail-Order Catalog, The, 110–11
Sears Prefabricated houses. See Prefabricated houses
Seasickness. See Ships
Seidlitz powder, 325
September 11, 2001 Attacks, 205, 229
Servants, 44, 113, 114, 325–31
Sesame Street, 288
Setup (Joke part), 15
Shandling, Gray, 42
Ships, 162–65
Silversmith, 16
Simpson, O.J., 281–83
Sixth Sense, The. See Titanic, The
Slavery, 331–35
Smartphones, 46, 49, 75, 89, 101, 118, 119, 142
Smith, Al (Politician), 226
Snow White and the Seven Dwarfs, 59
Some Enchanted Evening, 249
Someday my Prince Will Come (song), 59
South Pacific (musical), 249
Space Race, The, 254–57, 262
Space Shuttle. See Challenger, Space Shuttle
Spats (Footwear), 219–20
Spencer, Diana, 271
Spittoons, 124–26
Steam power, 41
Stove. See Wood-burning stove, See Gas stove
Sumeria, 16

T

Taft, William Howard, 227
Talking Machine. See Phonograph
Taximeter, 192
Tears in Heaven, 278–79
Telegraph. See Telegraphy
Telegraphy, 49–57
  Night rates, 55
  Singing telegram, 54
Telephones, 66–94, 107, 129, 324
  Car Phones, 92–93
  Connections, 88–89
  Early Days, 66–68
  Etiquette, 79–83
  Exchange Names, 76–77
  Landlines, 77–79
  Long Distance, 85–88
  Operators, 74–75
  Party Lines, 73–74
  Payphones, 89–92
  Phone Cords, 68
  Telephone Directories, 69–72
  Wrong Numbers, 83–85
Television, 94–101
  Cathode Ray Tubes, 96–98
  Color TV, 98–99
  Early Days, 94–96
  Future, 100–101
  Watching TV, 100
Television arrestor, 101

Texas (US State), 23, 241, 259, 260, 261, 280
Thaw, Henry. See Thaw/White Shooting, The
Thaw/White shooting, The, 215–16
The Bridge on the River Kwai, 235
The Exxon Valdez, 275–76
The River Kwai March. See Colonel Bogey March, The
Tipperary, Ireland, 218–19
Titanic, The, 217–18, 217–18
Tokyo, Japan, 88
Trains, 165–74, 184, 200, 201
Truman, Harry, 248–49
Turkey (Country), 34, 221
TV. See Television
Twain, Mark, 253
Twist, The (Dance), 260
Typewriter, 137–39

U

United States Prohibition, 84, 223–26
Urban legend
  German spotter, 243
  Ivory Soap, 309
  Skipping record, 134
Urban Legend
  Telephone off hook, 87
Urban legends
  The camera, 61

V

VCRs. See Videocassette Recorders
Videocassette Recorders, 139–41
Vietnam War, The, 257–59
Von Braun, Werner, 255

W

Waco, 192, 280
Wagon
  Chaise, 157
  Hansom, 193
  Hansom cabs, 192
Wagons, 156–60
  Tail board, 158
Wall Street Crash of 1929, 229
Ward, Artemis, 172
Werewolves of London (song), 268–69
Western Union, 56
White, Stanford. See Thaw/White Shooting, The
Wings (Band), 265
Wood, Natalie, 271–72
Wood-Burning Stove, 112–13
World War I, 34, 220–22, 259
World War II, 233–46, 290
  Adolf Hitler, 244
  D-Day, 243
  French Surrender, 236–37
  Goebbels, Joseph, 235
  Göring, Hermann, 235
  Himmler, Heinrich, 235
  Hirohito, 290
  Hitler, Adolf, 235, 233–36, 290
  Holocaust, The, 237–40
  Kamikaze Attacks, 241–43
  Mussolini, Benito, 290
  Post War, 243–46, 252
  Soldiers, 240–41

U-Boat, 252
War bonds, 291
Wright, Steven, 119

Y

Y2K, 283–84
Youth Subculture, 252–54
Yugo (car), 11

Z

Zevon, Warren. See Werewolves of London

www.ingramcontent.com/pod-product-compliance
Lightning Source LLC
LaVergne TN
LVHW091249110826
845146LV00002BA/578

* 9 7 9 8 9 9 4 9 1 6 5 1 3 *